FROM DESK TO DESTINATION

Escape Your Office, Work Anywhere,
and Live the Traveler's Dream

AARON B. CLEMENTS

Published by Cesar R. Espino / CRE Companies

From Desk to Destination / Aaron B. Clements – 1ST Ed.

ISBN: 978-1-960665-13-3 (dBook)
ISBN: 978-1-960665-14-0 (pbk)
ISBN: 978-1-960665-15-7 (Hard Cover)
ISBN: 978-1-960665-16-4 (Audio)

DEDICATION

This book is lovingly dedicated to my treasured niece, Trinity Noel Clements (2009-2022). Trinity was the true embodiment of love and joy; her radiant smile had the power to brighten the darkest of rooms, and her laughter was so contagiously delightful that it could lift anyone's spirits. She was a truly incredible and endearing soul, and her spirit embodied the heart of a warrior throughout her remarkable journey. Every day, I feel her absence, a void that can never be filled. Yet, I find solace in knowing that her legacy lives on, a shining beacon of hope and love.

Trinity's remarkable gift of organ donation is a testament to her extraordinary compassion. Through her final selfless act, she granted other children the precious gift of life, allowing them a chance at a brighter future. Her spirit endures in this act of heroism, and her memory lives on in the renewed lives of those she has touched.

My dearest Trin-Trin, your absence is felt deeply, and the world is dimmer without your light. You were and always will be, my Trincess, a unique and captivating soul who lives on in the hearts of those who knew and loved you. Until we meet again, your spirit will guide us, and your memory will continue to inspire us.

Proceeds from the sale of this book will go to the Juvenile Diabetes Research Foundation. If you feel compelled to make an additional contribution to the JDRF, helping prevent other families from enduring the heart-wrenching loss of a child due to this unrelenting illness, there is a simple yet powerful way to do so. By scanning the QR code below or visiting https://www.jdrf.org/donate/ you can embark on a journey of giving that could transform lives and bring hope to countless families battling juvenile/type 1 diabetes. Your generous donation will fund crucial research and provide support, resources, and a lifeline to families facing the same challenges that have touched our hearts. Together, we can be part of a movement that seeks to eradicate this devastating disease, ensuring a brighter, healthier future for children worldwide. Every dollar contributed through this QR code is a step toward a world where no family has to endure the tragedy of losing a child to this relentless disease. Your compassion and generosity can be a beacon of hope, illuminating the path to a better, healthier tomorrow. Scan the code now and join the fight against juvenile diabetes. Your support can make all the difference.

Additionally, Riley Cheer Guild is a volunteer auxiliary supporting patients and caregivers at Riley Hospital for Children, where Trinity received her care. They raise funds through various means to enhance hospital programs and provide comfort to families.

Sometimes that means bringing toys to children in their hospital room when they're unable to venture into the dedicated toy rooms throughout the facility. If you feel compelled to donate and support the Guild's mission to improve the hospital experience for patients and families, please do so by scanning the QR Code below or visit https://rileycheerguild.org/donate

CONTENTS

ACKNOWLEDGMENTS

Creating this book was a journey in and of itself. It took much more time, effort, and planning than I ever thought. As with any journey in life, there were ups and downs, twists and turns, and some unexpected speed bumps along the way, and it has turned out vastly different from what I had originally planned. I am incredibly thankful for the amazing people who made it possible. They include:

First and foremost, I want to thank my Mom, Vicki Deaver. She has always been a wonderful mother and role model to me growing up and remains my favorite person throughout adulthood. She provided me with the tools to build a life that I am proud of, and I am truly blessed to have such a sweet, caring, genuinely loving human being as my mom. I love you, mom, and I can't wait to share many more adventures together! I also want to thank my stepdad, Jay Deaver, for being such an incredible blessing to my mom and our family since he joined it. Thank you for supporting me at every turn and telling silly "Jayus" jokes along the way, even if I had already heard them. Have you heard the one about...? Yes. Yes, I have. I was the one who told you that joke in the first place.

I want to send a special thank you to Kelsey Bramer for her overwhelming support throughout this process. Thank you for taking the time out of your day, well days, to read all of the first drafts of the manuscript and provide me with your valuable feedback. I appreciate you helping me work through what to tweak, what to add, and even what to take out. Thank you for being an all-around awesome human and supporting my dreams and aspirations with this book and beyond. Even when we don't necessarily see things from the same perspective, you have been here to encourage me and help me keep moving forward. You are incredible.

I owe a debt of thanks to my friend and mentor, Marshall Sylver, without whom this book would be impossible. Thank you for inspiring me and guiding me on the path that led me to where this book and my first million would become a reality. Thank you for showing me what is possible in life and for supporting me and my aspirations. I am grateful to count you among my friends. I am especially grateful that you introduced me to my publisher, Cesar R. Espino, who inspired me to write a book and become an author in the first place by inviting me to be a part of his best-selling series, *You Can Overcome Anything*. Thank you, Cesar, for your support and for all the sleepless nights fueled by bilingual Karaoke and great times all over the country.

My gratitude goes out to my brothers, Allan II, Bobby, and Derick, and my sister, Heather, who helped mold me into who I am today. Thank you for teaching me about life growing up and showing me that family is important, even if we don't see each other as often as we would like. Thank you to my nieces and nephews, who are my legacy. I love you all and want you to know that you are an inspiration.

My Dad, Allan Clements I, was always a driving force in my life. Although you were taken from this world when I was an angst-riddled teen who didn't yet fully appreciate the value of family and creating lasting memories together, I appreciate you for being an amazing father and loving husband to Mom. You two showed me what real love was growing up. You taught me so much as a child and set a strong example of what a good human should be, and I appreciate you being a role model to me for that. You and Mom gave me the best childhood you knew how, and I am eternally grateful for that. I miss you every day and always aim to live my life in a manner that will make you proud.

Thank you to my adventure buddies who made the journeys exciting and unforgettable. Gregory Pepper (yes, that's his real name. We will leave his alias out at this time to protect the innocent or whatever), John Henry (yes, that is also his real name and no, I am not referring to the historic train guy, although I'm sure he was cool in his time as well), Aaron Venable with whom I started my first garage band in middle school (and we were wonderfully terrible) and with whom I still go on adventures with to this day, Blake and Justin Mattea (the original twins of evil before Zombie and Manson snagged it), Shannon Bradshaw and Olivia Melert (aka The Slushies), Eric Murto (thanks for the tour of the end of the world and the myriad NOLA adventures), Ashley Starry (the innocent victim), Jen Fall (I'm so proud that you learned to drive a van!), Brody Bell (the one and only DIY Corey Taylor), Jennifer Barnes (congrats on embracing and surviving the "Full Aaron Experience" through total spontaneity while traveling), Patrick Franzel (thanks for being my "head of security" when prompted), Lita (Lewis) Benefield, Ellen (Brooker) Walker, Angel Appel (thanks to you and Diedre for providing some semblance of sanity through the Covid deployments in IL), Jeremy, Nicole, and Bobbie Katherine Long (best three folks in SC), Joey and Betsy Longo (best couple in MD), Rob Morin, Evan Edbom, Jackie "Daniels" and The Buddies, Ashley, Krystal and Tracy Davis (the Davis Trifecta), "Big John" Sorrentino, Matt Puhy (nothing quite like a Puhy Party), Corina Alfaro (thanks for being an awesome Karaoke buddy), Christina Johnston (thanks for inviting me to be your rando roomie), Noah Baker, Frank and Sandra Aloia, Rhandi Kuchenmeister (Thanks for making the Bali dream a reality), Micah Whitney (the best purple cow in the whole Unites States), Tiffany Bernier, Colin Embree, Jocelyn Koesling (Bikini Girl), Robin Ervolina (my sister from another mister), Eric Teschke (Antarctica is going to be a blast), Jill Marentette (thanks for all the late night road trip conversations), Steve Feiler (thanks for all of the amazing food and Vegas adventures), Ryne Kentala, David Mast (thanks for all the snowboarding adventures and shared micheladas on the side of mountains), Carolyn Ferguson, Jordan Brill (thanks for not taking pictures of the 107 degree parking lot birthday nap), Jaclyn Lefebvre, Jake Allen, Andy and Nikki Koeltz, Andrea "Dre", Jenn Najar, Vin Paul, Tracy Nash, Jason and Kimmy Smith, Regis Salazar, DJ Barton, Noel Dinolfo, Hilary Lutes, and the rest of the PHX crew, Sara Jelinski, Raquel Pena, Ryan Bozza and Bridget Norman, Roscoe (I'm sure it's just around the next switchback) and Jarna Rainey, Beth Neff (thanks for jumping in on Burning Man on a whim a week before it began), AJ Puedan (King Kato), Michael and Zandra Moebius and Madeline and Ola and Anders and Anders and the rest of The Swedes, Julie Finch, Tony Csonka, Brad Jakubcanin, Tim Barton (R.I.P.) and Dicky LaReaux who make up The Leftovers, Chris and Meredith Warner and Dawn Adams (thanks for beginning the tradition of Line Wine), Rachel Kellenberger (cool prius - there, now somebody has said it), her amazing German partner in crime Lena Torke and Steve Ayers (we are proud of him for being alive), Yvette Teuffer (thanks for graciously inviting me to a different country for lunch), Becca Webb (who invented Brad on Warped Rewind), Matt Wolff, Mira Rosenzweig, Geoffrey, Elana and Gil Wartell, and so many, many more of my music cruise and adventure family across the globe and so many more that have made the adventures worth having.

Finally, I want to thank you, the readers. With your support, this book is worth writing. I hope you garner some valuable nuggets of wisdom, tips, and tricks from this book that enable and inspire you to begin your own incredible remote-work journey around the globe and make lasting memories that you will cherish forever!

INTRODUCTION

Are you tired of the same old routine? The daily grind of the nine-to-five, trapped in a cubicle, dreaming of escape? Well, my friend, it's time to break free from those chains and embark on a life-changing journey. Welcome to *"From Desk to Destination: Escape your office, Work Anywhere, and Live the Traveler's Dream."*

This book delves into the tantalizing allure of freedom, the sweet breeze of breaking free from the corporate grind. You'll discover the incredible benefits of quitting that desk job and embracing a remote work and travel lifestyle. But it's not just about escaping the office walls; it's about transforming your life and experiencing personal growth like never before.

Embracing remote work is the key to unlocking location independence, and we'll show you how to build a strong foundation for this exciting journey. You'll explore different remote work opportunities, from freelancing to remote employment and entrepreneurship. We'll help you assess your skills and identify remote-friendly careers, making that transition from a traditional office job smoother than ever.

Creating your portable office is essential for productivity on the go. We'll equip you with the necessary technology and tools to work remotely, whether it's a trusty laptop, a reliable internet connection, or efficient communication tools. You'll learn the art of setting up a productive workspace in various locations and discover invaluable strategies for managing time, staying organized, and maximizing your remote work productivity.

When it's time to unleash your wanderlust and plan your first adventure, we'll guide you in identifying your travel goals and aspirations and researching and selecting destinations suitable for remote work and travel. Organizing logistics such as visas, accommodations, and transportation will become a breeze, and we'll provide you with tips for creating a flexible itinerary that seamlessly combines work and adventure.

Before taking the leap into a remote lifestyle, we need to address those fears and doubts that may be holding us back. We'll share strategies for overcoming fear and embracing the unknown, helping you cultivate a positive mindset and build unshakable confidence in your decision.

As you embark on this thrilling adventure, finding that delicate balance between work and travel is crucial. We'll dive deep into establishing work-life boundaries and maintaining a healthy equilibrium. Discover strategies for managing work responsibilities while on the road, from effective time management to setting realistic expectations. You'll uncover tips for finding productive work environments, minimizing distractions, and the importance of self-discipline and accountability.

But what about the practicalities of being a digital nomad? Don't worry; we've got you covered with our digital nomad hacks. Learn what to pack and what to leave behind, strategies for finding suitable accommodations that cater to remote work, and essential tips for managing internet access and data plans while on the road. We'll even introduce you to tools and apps that make managing travel logistics, finances, and communications a breeze.

Of course, financial stability is crucial on this journey, and we'll help you navigate your finances like a pro. Establishing a budget for your remote work and travel lifestyle is essential, and we'll guide you through tracking expenses, managing finances on the road, and understanding the tax implications of this exciting lifestyle. You'll also discover the power of building financial independence and creating multiple income streams, paving the way for a truly fulfilling and sustainable adventure.

Once you're equipped with the basic knowledge and skills, we will help you shape your remote career. We'll explore remote work opportunities and industries suitable for location independence. Discover tips for finding remote job listings, utilizing online platforms, and building a freelance career or starting a remote business. Continuous learning and cultivating valuable skills in a remote work environment will become second nature.

But what happens when challenges and setbacks arise on this thrilling journey? Fear not! We'll arm you with strategies for overcoming common obstacles remote workers and travelers face. From tackling loneliness and cultural barriers to dealing with time zone differences, you'll be prepared for anything that comes your way. Drawing inspiration from stories of resilience and lessons learned, you'll find the strength and determination to conquer any hurdle.

From there, we'll explore the world's best remote work hubs. Highlighting popular destinations worldwide, we'll help you choose the perfect location based on factors such as cost of living, safety, and infrastructure. We'll also delve into the vibrant digital nomad communities and support networks in different locations, providing you with a sense of belonging and a network of like-minded individuals.

This journey isn't solely about work; it's about immersing yourself in different cultures. We'll guide you on embracing cultural immersion, connecting with local communities, and understanding their customs. You'll savor the authentic cuisine, partake in local traditions and festivals, and discover the joys of responsible tourism.

Are you worried about the costs? We'll share strategies for affordable adventures, ensuring you can travel on a budget without sacrificing experiences. From finding budget-friendly accommodations to saving money on transportation and maximizing your experiences while minimizing expenses, you'll become a master of frugal travel.

Now, slow down and savor the journey. We'll introduce you to the art of slow travel, where you can immerse yourself in destinations, discover hidden gems, and truly experience the beauty of each place. With our guidance, you'll learn to strike a perfect balance between work and leisure, ensuring a sustainable travel pace that allows you to make the most of every moment.

But this adventure isn't just about external experiences; it's about discovering yourself and undergoing personal growth and transformation. We'll encourage self-reflection and provide exercises to foster your personal development.

Finally, we'll tap into the power of bringing the adventure lifestyle home. We'll cover tools to empower you to embrace adventure in all aspects of your life.

So, my friend, are you ready to escape the confines of your office, work from anywhere, and live the traveler's dream? The adventure awaits, and *"From Desk to Destination"* is your ultimate guide. Let's embark on this transformative journey together!

CHAPTER ONE

THE CALL OF FREEDOM

Why Quitting your Desk Job and Traveling Matters

In today's fast-paced world, do you ever find yourself yearning for something more? Something beyond the routine of a desk job? I get it. We live in today's post-pandemic, interconnected world, so it's no wonder that many of us find ourselves yearning for something beyond the daily grind of a desk job. The allure of freedom is a powerful force. We all want to break free from the prison that is that office, to spread our wings and explore the world. Can you feel that longing deep within you? The call for freedom is like a siren song, pulling you away from the mundane and into a life of remote work and travel. Are you ready to answer that call?

Let's be real here. The corporate grind can be suffocating. The limited vacation time, the monotonous nine-to-five schedule, and the feeling of being trapped in a cubicle—it's enough to make anyone go insane. But here's the kicker: it doesn't have to be that way. There's a big, wide world out there, just waiting to be discovered, explored, experienced, and savored.

It's time to acknowledge the courage it takes to listen to that inner voice to honor our authentic desires. Deep down, we all yearn for lives that hold meaning and purpose. We want to feel alive and fulfilled, not merely going through the motions. So here's the truth, my friend: you have the power to create a life that aligns with your passions, values, and aspirations. That's where this remote work and travel lifestyle comes in. It offers us the opportunity to break free from the shackles of a conventional job and craft a life far beyond anything we have ever experienced. We crave a life where work becomes an extension of our passions, where we can weave our professional endeavors seamlessly with the joys of exploration. In the harmonious dance between work and travel, we can rewrite the rules and create a work-life blend that nourishes our souls and makes us come alive. Say goodbye to the soul-sucking 9-to-5 and hello to crafting a life that truly resonates with who you are.

Travel is the ultimate game-changer. It has this incredible ability to transform us on multiple levels. It's not just about hopping on a plane, ticking off destinations on a list, collecting passport stamps, and posting envy-inducing photos on social media; it's about diving headfirst into different cultures, traditions, and ways of life. It's about connecting with people from different walks of life, listening to their stories, expanding our understanding of the world, embracing the beauty of diversity, and discovering common threads that unite us all. It's about stepping into the unknown, challenging the status quo, and opening your mind to new perspectives. When you embrace travel, you're in for a wild ride of personal growth and self-discovery.

We find ourselves forever changed as we navigate new cultures, taste exotic flavors, and witness awe-inspiring landscapes. It's not just about visiting tourist spots and snapping selfies. It's about personal growth and discovering the best version of yourself. Stepping out of our comfort zones and immersing ourselves in unfamiliar environments can be daunting. But it's in those moments of discomfort that we truly find ourselves. We peel back the layers of who we think we are and uncover the depths of our true selves. Travel becomes a mirror, reflecting the beauty and complexity of strengths we never knew we had. We discover adaptability, resilience, and untapped potential within us that we didn't think possible. It's like diving into a sea of endless possibilities and coming out with a deeper understanding of who we are. It's almost like a personal development boot camp with stunning landscapes and delicious food. Get ready for a wild ride!

Embracing the call of freedom and pursuing a remote work and travel lifestyle isn't always an easy path. Living life on your own terms and traveling the world won't always be a walk in the park. There will be hurdles to overcome, no doubt about it. It requires courage, adaptability, and a willingness to embrace uncertainty. There will be challenges and moments of doubt along the way, but the rewards that await you are immeasurable.

In the face of these challenges, you have the opportunity to cultivate resilience, tap into your inner courage, and dare greatly. You'll unlock a sense of freedom and possibility you may have never known. You'll create memories that will last a lifetime. And hey, the incredible people you'll meet along the way? They'll inspire and enrich your life in ways you can't even imagine. Travel is about human connection, about opening our hearts to the beauty of diversity and shared experiences. It is about cultivating empathy, compassion, and understanding for our fellow global citizens. Through travel, we weave a tapestry of shared stories, building bridges that unite us as one human family.

So, my friend, if you hear that call of freedom resonating within you, don't ignore it. Embrace it with open arms! Take the leap of faith, quit that desk job, pack your bags, and embark on the adventure of a lifetime. Get ready for this epic journey of working remotely and living the traveler's dream in a world full of wonder. Sure, it won't always be easy, but the rewards will be worth it. The growth, joy, and fulfillment that await you on the other side are worth every ounce of effort.

Are you ready to answer the call of freedom and thrive in this game of life? I know you've got what it takes. Together, we'll delve into the actionable steps, real-world insights, and helpful strategies that will empower you on this extraordinary journey of quitting your desk job, embracing remote work, and living an incredible life of adventure. It's time to break free from the shackles of your desk job and live life like a freakin' rockstar!

CHAPTER TWO

EMBRACING REMOTE WORK

Building a Strong Foundation for Location Independence

In a world obsessed with conventional definitions of success, it's time for us to have a little heart-to-heart conversation. Welcome, my fellow adventurer, to the transformative journey of embracing remote work! Let's challenge the status quo and explore what true location independence really means to us. It's an exciting journey that allows you to liberate yourself from the constraints of the traditional office, forge a path that's uniquely yours, and step into a realm of limitless possibilities. Are you ready to redefine success, build work-life harmony that aligns with your values and passions, and dive head-first into the adventurer's world of remote work and travel? Let's roll up our sleeves, explore the various opportunities available, assess your skills, and build a rock-solid foundation for your journey to location independence. Get ready to experience a new level of freedom and fulfillment!

Let's dive in and unravel the myths that society has ingrained in us. Success is not solely defined by climbing the corporate ladder or accumulating material possessions. It's about finding fulfillment, purpose, and joy in every aspect of our lives. It's about creating a harmonious balance between our work, relationships, personal growth, and our adventures on the road.

We live in a culture that often measures success by external markers—job titles, salaries, and social status. Traditional notions of success often revolve around climbing the corporate ladder and chasing promotions to finally land that big corner office with a spectacular view of the city. But what if success meant something different for us? What if it meant finding work that aligns with our values, allows us to make an impact, and gives us the freedom to live on our own terms? Here's the truth, my friend: true success is an inside job. It's about connecting with our authentic selves, understanding our core values, and aligning our actions with what truly matters to us. It's about living a life that reflects our unique purpose and positively impacts the world around us. It's time to explore remote work opportunities and other alternative paths that can provide financial stability and the flexibility to pursue our passions and travel the world. Our office can be in any corner of the world with a spectacular view of whatever city we choose from day to day!

To embark on a successful remote work journey, aligning your skills and passions with careers that thrive in this realm is crucial. Take the time to explore your talents, strengths, and areas of expertise. Consider how these abilities can be applied to remote-friendly industries and professions. Whether you excel in technology, creative arts, or communication, remote work opportunities are eagerly awaiting your unique contribution. Think of it as a game of match-making, where we find that sweet spot where your talents and interests intersect with remote work opportunities.

What are your passions? What are you naturally good at? What things make you do a happy dance? Identify areas where your skills align with remote-friendly careers and explore opportunities in those industries and professions. From digital marketing and web development to writing and coaching, countless opportunities exist to build a fulfilling career remotely. It's all about finding the perfect fit for you. Let's find the sweet spot where your skills align with remote-friendly careers. Whether you're a coding wizard, creative wordsmith, or problem-solving guru, a world of opportunities is waiting for you. By matching your talents with the right opportunities, you can forge a fulfilling and financially rewarding path.

Making the leap from the structured office environment to the boundless realm of remote work can feel like embarking on an exciting yet uncertain adventure into the unknown. Understand the challenges and benefits of the transition. It's a shift that requires creativity and a whole new mindset. It's a chance to break free from the traditional mold and embrace a new working method that offers flexibility, autonomy, and limitless possibilities. Adaptation and discipline are going to be your best friends on this journey.

Now, let's dive into some practical strategies to navigate this transition successfully. To start, you need to set yourself up for success by creating a designated workspace that fuels your inspiration and productivity, free from distractions. A special place where you can immerse yourself in your work fully. Find a spot where you can focus without distractions, whether it's a cozy corner in your home or a stylish cafe or coffee shop that becomes your remote office; find a space that sparks your creativity and allows you to immerse yourself in your work fully.

Note that it's not just about the physical environment. Time management is key in the realm of remote work because you're no longer tied to the 9-to-5 grind. Learn to master your schedule, prioritize tasks, and stay focused amidst the endless distractions that can tempt you away from your goals. You'll maximize productivity and make the most of this newfound freedom by harnessing your time effectively.

Speaking of freedom, balance is vital as you embark on this location-independent adventure. Remote work can blur the lines between your professional and personal time. Establish clear boundaries between work and your personal life to maintain your sanity and preserve the harmony of both worlds. Set some ground rules and abide by them to keep that harmony intact. Create a schedule, communicate your availability to others, and don't forget to take breaks to recharge and enjoy the adventure. Develop rituals and routines that help you switch gears and recharge to bring your best self to both realms.

Now that we've covered the practical side of things, let's talk about the mindset shift. Our beliefs, thoughts, and self-talk shape our reality. Embrace the freedom and the opportunity to explore uncharted territories to push the boundaries of what's possible. Let go of any fears or doubts that may hold you back and embrace the unknown with enthusiasm and curiosity. Rid yourself of limiting beliefs and embrace a growth mindset that sees challenges as opportunities, failures as learning experiences, and setbacks as stepping stones toward success. It's about cultivating self-compassion, celebrating progress, and embracing the journey rather than fixating solely on any single destination.

Remote work opens up a world of possibilities full of open doors to endless growth and personal development, so embrace it fully. Take advantage of the flexibility and explore new horizons. You can work from the beach, the mountains, a rooftop terrace, or anywhere in between. Enveloping yourself in the remote work lifestyle is an opportunity to design a life that aligns with your dreams and aspirations. You can forge a path that leads to true fulfillment and financial abundance through self-reflection, skill assessment, and embracing new possibilities. Believe in yourself, seize the opportunities that come your way, and let your remote work journey unfold with purpose and determination. This journey will empower you to design your own path and invite you to cultivate a deeper connection with yourself and the world around you. Remember, you have the power within you to create the life you envision, and let the magic unfold!

Embrace the power of the digital world. Welcome to the digital stage! Understand the importance of building an online presence and creating a personal brand that showcases your skills, expertise, and unique value proposition. Learn how to optimize your online profiles, create a compelling portfolio or website, and utilize social media platforms to network, connect with potential clients or employers, and showcase your work. Think of social media as your megaphone—a platform to share insights, engage with your audience, and build meaningful relationships. It's about amplifying your voice, showcasing your expertise, and connecting with like-minded individuals who can propel your remote work journey forward.

In today's digital landscape, having a strong, robust online presence is like having a superhero cape—it sets you apart from the crowd. Invest time in creating a compelling online presence through social media, professional networking platforms, and even a personal website or portfolio. Share your knowledge, engage with others, and position yourself as an authority in your field. By cultivating a solid online presence, you open doors to collaboration, growth, and visibility in the remote work landscape. Shine your brightest online and create a personal brand that captures your unique essence. It's time to let the world know you mean business!

Remember, transitioning from a traditional office to remote work may come with its fair share of challenges. Still, with the right mindset, strategies, and a little dose of unwavering belief in yourself, you'll hit the ground running in this new remote work adventure. Let's explore the diverse paths that can lead you to the fulfillment and freedom you desire. In the next few chapters, we will build a launch pad for your remote work lifestyle by analyzing the incredible array of opportunities available by examining the three major categories of remote work opportunities: Freelancing, Remote Employment, and Entrepreneurship. So buckle up and get ready to seize the day and make your mark in this exciting new frontier!

CHAPTER THREE

———

FREELANCING

Embracing Autonomy and Building a Thriving Career

Freelancing: Discover the freedom and flexibility of being your own boss, working on projects you love, and calling the shots. It's all about building your personal brand, attracting clients, and delivering top-notch work to clients who appreciate your expertise. Imagine being the captain of your own ship, charting your course, and sailing toward success. Explore the world of freelance gigs, where you can offer your skills and expertise to clients from around the globe. As a freelancer, you have the autonomy to curate a portfolio of projects that ignite your passion and align with your values. You're in control, my friend.

Let's explore a few examples of potentially thrilling and rewarding freelance adventures that could prove to be highly lucrative:

Copywriting: Are you a wordsmith with a knack for persuasion? Copywriting could be your golden ticket! Unleash the power of your words and master the art of persuasion. Help businesses craft compelling sales pages, engaging blog posts, and captivating ad copy. Your writing skills can drive sales and conversions. Your words can have the power to drive sales and conversions, making you a sought-after freelance copywriter.

Web Development: In this digital age, businesses always need talented web developers. Step into the digital realm and become a web development virtuoso. With coding skills and the ability to create stunning websites, businesses will flock to you. If you do not yet have coding skills, there are myriad online courses and coding schools that you can enroll in to begin your coding journey today. Once you learn to master the art of web development, you will be in high demand. Build user-friendly and visually appealing websites for clients, and watch your freelance career soar to new heights.

Graphic Design: Do you have an eye for aesthetics and a creative flair? Embrace your creativity and harness the visual language of design. From logos to social media graphics, businesses crave captivating visuals that make them stand out. Use your design skills and aesthetic eye to create eye-catching artwork, and watch as freelance gigs pour in.

Video Editing: With the rise of YouTube and social media, video content is more popular than ever. If you have a knack for storytelling and can bring footage to life through editing, video editing could be your path to freelance success. Dive into the world of visual storytelling and bring footage to life. As a video editing maestro, you'll help clients create stunning, engaging videos that captivate their audience. Ride the wave of YouTube and social media's popularity and surf to freelance success.

Social Media Management: Are you a social media whiz? Businesses are always looking for skilled social media managers who can grow their online presence. Command the social media landscape with your expertise. Develop engaging content, interact with followers, and strategize to increase brand visibility and engagement.

Online Coaching or Consulting: Are you an expert in a specific field? Use your knowledge and experience to offer online coaching or consulting services. Share your expert knowledge and guide others to success. Whether it's business, fitness, or personal development, there's always a demand for expert guidance. Offer online coaching or consulting services to help others achieve their goals and watch your freelance income flourish.

Content Writing: If you love to write and have a way with words, content writing is your gateway to a lucrative freelance career. Let your words shape industries and captivate readers. Create engaging blog posts, informative articles, and SEO-optimized website content for clients. Your writing skills can open doors to a wide range of industries and opportunities.

Virtual Assistance: Busy entrepreneurs and businesses often need extra hands to handle administrative tasks. Be the reliable support entrepreneurs and business professionals need to thrive. As a virtual assistant, you can tackle administrative tasks and keep businesses organized by providing support with scheduling, email management, research, and more. Help clients stay on track and focused while enjoying the flexibility of remote work.

Translation Services: Fluency in multiple languages can be a valuable asset. Offer your services as a freelance translator and help businesses break through language barriers and connect the world. Your fluency in multiple languages is a priceless asset. Translating documents and websites or even acting as an interpreter can be lucrative for those with language skills. Extend your valuable expertise as a freelance translator, bridging gaps and facilitating business communication.

E-commerce Store Setup and Management: With the rise of online shopping, businesses need help setting up and managing their e-commerce stores. Capitalize on the booming world of online shopping. If you're tech-savvy and familiar with platforms like Shopify or WooCommerce, provide your specialized services to assist businesses and individual customers with store setup, product listings, and online presence optimization.

These are just a few examples of highly lucrative freelance gigs that can be done from anywhere. The key is identifying your unique strengths and skills, allowing you to find your niche in the vast freelance landscape and delivering exceptional work to your clients. Another avenue to explore is the world of freelancing platforms like Upwork and Freelancer. These platforms connect freelancers with clients looking for their specific skills. It's like an online marketplace where you can showcase your talents and get paid for your expertise. Create a compelling profile, highlight your strengths, and bid on projects that align with your skills. It's like opening up your own shop in a busy market square, attracting clients from far and wide. Armed with determination and a dash of creativity, deliver exceptional work to your clients, like a virtuoso performing a masterpiece. Watch as your freelance career transforms into a thriving and fulfilling adventure, where each project becomes a new chapter in your success story.

CHAPTER FOUR

REMOTE EMPLOYMENT

Finding Stability and Flexibility in a Virtual World

Remote employment: Imagine working for a company that values your talent and lets you do your thing from wherever you please. Envision yourself as part of a progressive organization that values flexibility and embraces remote work. With remote employment, you can say goodbye to that dreaded commute, leverage your talents, and contribute to a team while embracing the freedom of working from anywhere in the world. Explore the growing trend of remote jobs offered by companies that allow you to work from anywhere. It's an opportunity to combine stability and flexibility to suit your lifestyle, so it's a win-win! Discover how to find remote job listings and position yourself as a strong candidate.

Let's dive deep into the treasure trove of resources for finding remote employment.

First and foremost, we have the mighty LinkedIn. This digital arena is the pinnacle of social media for professionals looking to connect, share their expertise, connect with like-minded folks, uncover golden opportunities, and even find remote job opportunities. Build a strong profile, connect with influencers in your desired field, and engage in meaningful discussions. It's like having a backstage pass to the job market where you can pop into a virtual greenroom filled with potential collaborators and employers.

Now, let's talk about professional communities and forums. Engage on platforms like Reddit and Quora, where industry insights flow freely. They are virtual meeting grounds where professionals gather to share valuable perspectives and discuss industry trends. It's like entering a room filled with experts sharing their wisdom. Engage in conversations, ask questions, and showcase your expertise. Subreddits on Reddit like r/forhire and r/remotejobs are teeming with remote work listings. You might stumble upon job openings or make valuable connections that can lead you to remote employment riches.

Moving onto job-search-specific websites, you have gems like FlexJobs and Remote.co. These sites are like treasure chests filled with remote job listings. They do the heavy lifting for you, filtering out all the junk and presenting you with the cream of the crop. It's like having a personal job-hunting assistant, minus the coffee runs. When utilizing larger employment-related search engines such as Indeed and Glassdoor, bear in mind that those platforms scour the vast internet, gathering job listings from all corners of the web, but they are not focused on remote work specifically, so you will need to be strategic with your search terms. That said, niche job boards like Remote OK, We Work Remotely, and Virtual Vocations offer curated remote job opportunities. They're like hidden treasure maps guiding you to remote employment riches.

Websites like Remote Year and Remote Work Hub cater exclusively to gathering companies that are all about remote work. Their business model is driven by providing services for remote workers, so they make it easy for you to become one of their customers by helping you find remote work opportunities. It's like stepping into an exclusive lounge where you can connect with businesses embracing the remote revolution.

Online communities: Let's talk about the power of connections. It's like hanging out at a virtual water cooler buzzing with insights, job leads, and opportunities.

Industry-specific websites: Are you a tech whiz or a creative genius? Well, there are websites tailored just for you. Check out 10x Management for tech and creative gigs or Idealist for nonprofit remote opportunities. It's like stumbling upon the holy grail of remote work, perfectly tailored to your unique skills.

Let's not forget the power of good old-fashioned networking. Contact your connections, join online communities, and attend virtual conferences, webinars, and industry events. Rub shoulders with professionals in your field, exchange contact information, and nurture those connections. You never know who might have the hookup to your dream remote gig. It's like building a network of allies who support and uplift you on your quest for remote employment greatness.

Tap into the power of social media. Platforms like Twitter and Facebook have job groups and pages dedicated to remote work and freelancing that are bustling with job postings, industry news, and discussions. Join Facebook groups like "Digital Nomad Jobs" or "Remote Workers Worldwide" to tap into a vibrant network of like-minded individuals. Scroll through those feeds, engage with fellow professionals, and tell the world about your expertise. Giving more than you take is the key to getting the most from these groups. Do your best to add value to the individuals in the group and the group as a whole. It's like standing on a digital soapbox, captivating the attention of potential employers with your knowledge and charisma. You might find a sweet remote gig while scrolling through cute cat videos. It's a win-win!

Last but certainly not least, have a conversation with your current company about what remote opportunities are available or even if the role that you are currently in can be shifted to a fully remote position. One of the few good things to come out of the pandemic-era world is the fact that technology advanced extremely quickly to allow for a vast majority of jobs to be adapted to a remote work scenario. If you are one of the unfortunate masses who have returned to the office setting completely, maybe now is the right time for you to talk with your team about making the remote transition permanent.

When you have proven that you can be effective at your role in a fully remote work environment, it would be worth your while to have the conversation. If they are not receptive to the idea, then continue your search outside of your current team/role/company. Still, you might be surprised at their willingness to make the accommodation in lieu of losing a well-trained and highly effective employee who has been with them for a while. The major advantage for you with this strategy is that you will be able to skip the job hunt altogether. The answer to every question you don't ask is no, so you may as well ask.

Remember, the remote job market is vast and ever-changing. Perseverance and resourcefulness are the keys to unlocking remote employment success, so keep your eyes peeled, be proactive, and stay hungry for those opportunities. Harness the power of these resources, master your craft, and present yourself as an irresistible asset to potential employers. Napoleon Hill would have told you that the world is filled with opportunities for those who seek them. Now, go forth and claim your remote employment destiny!

CHAPTER FIVE

———

ENTREPRENEURSHIP

Turning Ideas into Reality and Creating Impact

Entrepreneurship: Have you ever dreamed of starting your own business? Picture the exhilaration of building your own enterprise from scratch, where you can shape your destiny and create a lasting impact by turning your ideas into reality. Get ready to unleash your inner entrepreneurial spirit and watch it soar. We're talking about taking your passion, ideas, and skills and turning them into a thriving business free of dependency on location. As an entrepreneur in the remote workspace, you have the freedom to unleash your creativity, innovate, and solve meaningful problems. Together, we'll explore how you can leverage technology to build a business that can be operated remotely. You become the captain of your ship, navigating the turbulent waters of entrepreneurship and steering toward success. Where do you want to go first?

If you're ready to dive into the wild world of entrepreneurship, strap yourself in because we're about to embark on a profound and chaotic journey. Becoming an entrepreneur is not for the faint of heart—it requires courage, determination, and a burning desire to achieve greatness. It's like strapping yourself into a roller coaster ride with no seatbelt—it's thrilling, unpredictable, and full of ups and downs. But hey, if you're willing to embrace the chaos and put in the work, the rewards can be mind-blowing.

First things first, you have to find your passion. What sets your soul on fire? What makes you jump out of bed in the morning? What makes you come alive? What stirs your deepest emotions? Discover that thing that gets your heart racing, and you're off to a great start. Unearthing your true purpose is the foundation upon which your entrepreneurial empire shall be built. It could be anything from creating art to solving complex societal problems, creating innovative products, revolutionizing an industry, or even selling wacky gadgets. The key is to do what you love and love what you do. Your passion will be the driving force that propels you forward.

Once you've found your passion, it's time to get your hustle on and delve into the art of strategic planning. Yeah, that's right, you must hustle like a hungry cheetah chasing its prey. Vision without action is merely a daydream. Put in the hours, grind it out, and don't be afraid to get your hands dirty. Develop a crystal-clear vision of where you want to go and then craft a detailed roadmap. Break down your big goals into smaller, actionable steps, and consistently work toward them with unwavering focus. Success doesn't come knocking on your door while sitting on the couch watching TV. You have to go out there and make things happen. Remember, every successful endeavor begins with a well-thought-out plan.

Now, here's where things get interesting—you must take risks. Entrepreneurship is all about stepping outside your comfort zone and taking leaps of faith. It's like jumping off a cliff and building your plane as you fly it. Yeah, it sounds scary, but that's where the magic happens. Embrace the unknown, learn from failure, and keep pushing forward.

Lean fully into the power of unwavering persistence and relentless determination. As an entrepreneur, you will face countless obstacles and setbacks along the way. But here's the secret: every setback is a steppingstone to success. Embrace failure as a valuable teacher, and let persistence be your guiding light. Mistakes are proof that you are putting forth effort. Pick yourself up, forge ahead with unyielding determination, and you will conquer mountains that others deem impossible.

Next up, surround yourself with the right people and yield to the strength of a mastermind alliance. You need a tribe of like-minded individuals who lift you, challenge you, believe in your crazy dreams, and share your passion for growth and success. Seek mentors, collaborators, and advisors who can guide and inspire you on your entrepreneurial journey. Connect with fellow entrepreneurs and build a network that inspires and supports you. Remember, you're the average of the people you hang out with, so choose wisely. Together, you will form an unstoppable force where the collective wisdom and support allow everyone to lift as they grow.

Continual self-improvement is the fuel that propels the engine of success. Stay hungry for knowledge. Read books, listen to podcasts, attend seminars—soak up every ounce of wisdom you can find. Enroll and engage in courses that expand your horizons and deepen your understanding. The more you learn, the more tools you'll have in your entrepreneurial toolkit. And remember, education isn't just about formal schooling. Some of the greatest lessons are learned through real-life experiences. Cultivate the mindset of a lifelong learner, as it is through constant growth that you unlock your true potential.

As an entrepreneur, it is crucial to develop the art of decision-making. Embrace the responsibility of making choices that shape the trajectory of your business. Analyze the available information, seek counsel from trusted advisors, and then make swift, confident decisions. Remember, indecision is the enemy of progress. Trust your instincts and dare to take calculated risks.

Lastly, stay true to yourself and let your character shine like a beacon of integrity. Don't get caught up in chasing someone else's version of success. This journey is about discovering your path and unique flavor of awesomeness. Be authentic, be genuine, and conduct your business affairs with honesty, transparency, and a genuine desire to serve others. When you stay true to yourself, you attract the right opportunities and people into your life. Build a reputation based on trust and reliability, for it is the cornerstone on which lasting success is built. Uphold your values, even in the face of temptation, and you will attract loyal customers and partners who resonate with your authentic spirit.

So, if you're ready to embark on this crazy entrepreneurial adventure, remember to unleash your passion, create a strategic roadmap, hustle like a beast, take risks, embrace failure as a teacher, surround yourself with the right tribe, never stop learning, and stay true to who you are. The entrepreneurial path is paved with passion, planning, persistence, and personal growth. With these principles as your guide, you'll navigate the labyrinth of entrepreneurship and emerge on top. It's going to be a wild ride, but trust me, the journey is worth it. Now, go out there and conquer the world with your indomitable spirit!

CHAPTER SIX

CREATING YOUR PORTABLE OFFICE

Essential Tools and Strategies for Working Remotely

Welcome to the world of remote work, where your office becomes portable and the possibilities for success are limitless. In this chapter, we'll dive deep into the essential tools and strategies that will propel your remote work experience to new heights and help you construct a productive and harmonious remote work setup. Get ready to optimize your productivity, conquer your goals, and make the most of this remarkable lifestyle. Prepare to unlock the keys to remote work excellence and create a portable office that fosters both personal and professional growth. Let's dive in, shall we?

Picture this: your laptop, reliable internet connection, and a world of opportunities at your fingertips. Remote work gives you the freedom to choose where and how you work, and to truly thrive, you need to equip yourself with the right tools and embrace effective strategies.

A reliable laptop or computer: Seek out a device that meets

your specific needs, providing the processing power, storage capacity, versatility, and mobility required for ideal remote work conditions. Whether that be a system optimized for crunching numbers, designing masterpieces, or anything in between, invest in a device that aligns with your needs and ensures a seamless work experience.

A steadfast internet connection: Let's face it, a reliable internet connection is your gateway to the virtual world, and it is the lifeline of your remote work operations. It is indispensable for seamless communication, information access, and collaboration. Without a reliable internet connection, your remote work dreams can quickly become a nightmare. A robust connection enables you to connect with colleagues, clients, and a world of opportunities. Ensure you have access to a stable and high-speed connection to stay engaged in the virtual realm.

Communication tools that fuel collaboration: Explore various communication tools, from email platforms to video conferencing platforms or project management software. Leverage the tools that align with your workflow and facilitate seamless communication and collaboration with your team and clients. Embrace the power of effective communication and digital connectivity to transcend physical distances and establish strong virtual connections.

Tips for setting up a productive workspace in various locations:

One of the joys of remote work is the ability to work from anywhere. However, creating a conducive and inspiring workspace is vital for maintaining focus, motivation, productivity, and a sense of balance in your remote work environment. Consider the following tips to establish a productive and inspiring workspace no matter where you find yourself:

Choose your surroundings wisely: Find a location that inspires and energizes you. It could be a dedicated home office, a bustling coffee shop, or a serene coworking space. Select an environment that fosters focus, creativity, and motivation. Find your sweet spot and let the environment fuel your productivity.

Squirrel! Minimize distractions and optimize focus: Remote work may present unique distractions, ranging from household responsibilities to the allure of social media. Identify potential pitfalls and take proactive steps to minimize their impact. Implement strategies to reduce distractions, establish boundaries, and cultivate an environment that enables deep work and sustained concentration. Whether it's turning off notifications, using noise-canceling headphones, or setting boundaries with family members, friends, or roommates, create an environment that allows you to be fully present and concentrate on your tasks.

Ergonomics matter: Create a physically comfortable and ergonomic setup. Prioritize your physical well-being by setting up an ergonomic workspace. Invest in a comfortable, ergonomic chair, position your computer screen at eye level, and incorporate movement breaks when designing a dedicated home office. Physical comfort is crucial in enhancing your mental focus and productivity. Set up adequate lighting and organize your workspace to promote proper posture and minimize strain and fatigue. A comfortable and ergonomic setup will enhance your overall well-being and support long hours of productive work.

Strategies for managing time and staying organized while working remotely:

With the freedom of remote work comes the responsibility to manage yourself. Effective time management and organizational skills are your secret weapons for success in the remote work landscape. Explore the following strategies to optimize your productivity and maintain a sense of order in your remote work routine:

Craft a well-defined personalized routine: Experiment with different routines to cultivate a structured system that suits your natural rhythms and aligns with your productivity patterns. Establish dedicated blocks of time for focused work, breaks, personal activities, and self-care. A consistent routine will provide structure and help you maintain balance in your remote work lifestyle.

Prioritize tasks with clarity and intention: Identify your most important tasks and allocate dedicated time to tackle them head-on. Consider adopting strategies such as Eisenhower's matrix, time blocking, ABC prioritization, or the Pomodoro technique to ensure that you are consistently focusing on high-value activities that align with your goals and deliver maximum impact. By focusing on high-priority items first, you can make substantial progress and avoid getting overwhelmed by the sheer volume of work.

Leverage digital tools for organization and productivity: Harness the power of digital tools, such as project management software, task management applications, and calendar systems, to streamline your workflow, track deadlines, and manage your tasks effectively. These tools can help you stay organized, collaborate with others, and maintain clarity amidst multiple responsibilities. Embrace the power of automation and synchronization to streamline your workflow, enhance productivity, and ensure nothing falls through the cracks.

Remote work productivity hacks and techniques:

When it comes to productivity, everyone has their unique hacks and techniques. Unlocking your full potential in the realm of remote work requires adopting proven productivity hacks and techniques that align with your unique strengths and preferences. Consider the following strategies to supercharge your productivity, elevate your performance, and achieve remarkable results:

Embrace deep work and master the art of single-tasking: In an age of constant distractions, the ability to engage in deep work is a superpower. Carve out focused blocks of time, eliminate distractions, and immerse yourself fully in a single task. Contrary to popular belief, multitasking can hinder productivity. Focus on one task at a time instead of spreading yourself thin across multiple tasks. Give that one task your undivided attention and watch your efficiency skyrocket. You'll be amazed at how much more you can accomplish when you fully immerse yourself in each activity. By dedicating your focus to a single action item, deliverable, or project, you will achieve higher productivity levels and creative output.

Embrace flexibility and strategic breaks: Remote work allows flexibility in how and when you work. Taking breaks isn't a sign of laziness; it's crucial to maintaining productivity. Discover and leverage your peak productivity hours to accomplish your most critical tasks. Recognize the importance of rest and rejuvenation in sustaining long-term productivity. Incorporate short breaks throughout your day to recharge your energy and clear your mind. Use these breaks to stretch, go for a walk, or engage in activities that nourish your soul so you can return to your work with renewed focus and clarity.

Embrace a healthy work-life integration that aligns with your values and personal needs. Stepping away from your work, even briefly, can provide a fresh perspective and recharge your creative energies. You might consider exploring the Pomodoro Technique: Break your work into focused intervals, typically 25 minutes, followed by short breaks. This technique promotes productivity by capitalizing on short bursts of intense focus, allowing you to maintain high energy levels and avoid burnout.

Pursue self-discipline and accountability: Remote work demands high discipline and self-accountability. Without the watchful eyes of coworkers and supervisors, it's easy to fall into the procrastination trap. Stay disciplined, set goals, and hold yourself accountable. Cultivate habits and routines that reinforce your commitment to excellence, and embrace the intrinsic motivation that comes from aligning your work with your values and ambitions. Find your inner drive and let it push you toward excellence.

Implement the power of visualization and goal-setting: Visualize your desired outcomes, set clear goals, and break them down into actionable steps. Visualizing success and working toward specific objectives fuels motivation, enhances focus, and propels you toward accomplishing your aspirations.

Internalize a growth mindset and continuous learning: Adopt a growth mindset, viewing challenges as opportunities for growth and embracing a continuous learning mindset. Actively seek new knowledge, acquire new skills, and remain adaptable and open to change. An attitude centered on growth will fuel your personal and professional development.

Implementing these essential strategies for creating your portable office, utilizing the necessary technology, designing a productive workspace, managing your time effectively, and embracing productivity-boosting techniques will pave the way for a remarkable remote work experience. Embrace the flexibility and possibilities that remote work offers, and let it propel you toward achieving your goals and aspirations. Prepare to thrive in this new era of work, where boundaries disappear and success knows no limits.

CHAPTER SEVEN

UNLEASHING YOUR WANDERLUST

Planning Your First Adventure

We're about to embark on a journey of epic proportions as we break down everything you need to know to ignite your wanderlust and set the stage for a life-changing experience as you turn your remote work dreams into a reality. Get ready to transform your aspirations into a well-crafted plan that will set you on a path of thrilling exploration that will guide you toward remarkable destinations and extraordinary discoveries.

First, let's begin by clearly identifying your travel goals and aspirations. What do you crave? Is it the allure of ancient civilizations, the enchantment of vibrant cityscapes, or the tranquility of untouched natural wonders? What gets your heart pumping with excitement? Is it the thought of soaking up the sun on a pristine beach, immersing yourself in a bustling metropolis, or finding solace in the serene beauty of remote mountain hideaways? What ignites your curiosity and fills you with a sense of adventure? Perhaps it is the desire to immerse yourself in diverse cultures, savoring the flavors of new cuisines? Take a moment to close your eyes and envision yourself in these destinations, soaking in the atmosphere, embracing the adventure that awaits, and letting your imagination run wild. Defining your travel goals with pristine clarity lays the foundation for an adventure that aligns perfectly with your passions and desires. It's time to give shape to your dreams.

Next up, it's time to do some good old-fashioned research. This is where you become a detective, uncovering the hidden gems that will make your journey extraordinary. Dive into the depths of the internet, scour travel websites and blogs, and devour travel guides. Chat with fellow adventurers to tap into the collective wisdom of explorers who have walked the path before you. Learn from their experiences, unearth hidden gems, and discover the perfect destinations that align with your remote work needs. Look for places that offer reliable Wi-Fi, vibrant coworking spaces, and a community of like-minded digital nomads. Through diligent research, seek out destinations that not only cater to remote work but also offer unique experiences that align with your passions, captivating cultural experiences, breathtaking landscapes, and the potential for personal growth. Within these hidden gems, you will find the magic and authenticity that will make your adventure truly unforgettable.

One valuable piece of advice to help you navigate your adventure seamlessly is to embrace the importance of creating a flexible itinerary. As a remote worker, you have the privilege of blending work and exploration. While planning is essential, leave room for spontaneity and unexpected encounters. Embrace the freedom that comes with remote work and allow yourself to be guided by the serendipitous opportunities that present themselves. Embrace the freedom to adapt your schedule and make room for unexpected discoveries along the way that unveil the true essence of a destination. Allow yourself to immerse in local cultures, try new cuisines, and venture off the beaten path. Remember, it is often in the unplanned moments that the most profound experiences unfold.

As you progress, bring the logistics of your journey into focus. Navigating the complexities of visas, accommodations, and transportation requires attention to detail and strategic planning. Familiarize yourself with the visa requirements of your chosen destinations and plan accordingly, ensuring that you have all the necessary documents in order and that you have a thorough understanding of the necessary processes involved. Seek out accommodations that cater to remote workers, striking a balance between comfort, connectivity, and affordability. Whether it be boutique hotels, co-living spaces, or unique homestays with work-friendly setups, choose accommodations that enhance your experience and provide a conducive environment for work and exploration. And when it comes to transportation, think outside the box. Consider options that align with your travel style and suit your adventurous spirit. Be it hopping on a local bus or train, renting a car, bike, or scooter, or embracing the freedom of a nomadic lifestyle in a campervan. Research local healthcare facilities and familiarize yourself with emergency contacts. The world is your playground, and by attending to these details in advance, you'll ensure peace of mind and create a solid foundation for your travels.

Remember, planning your first remote work and travel adventure should be exciting and empowering. Embrace the unknown, trust your intuition, and approach this journey with an open heart and mind. To help you navigate the process of selecting destinations and organizing logistics, consider the following resources and tips to guide you along the way:

Travel websites and blogs: Explore popular travel websites and blogs dedicated to remote work and digital nomad lifestyles. These platforms, where seasoned travelers share their personal experiences and recommendations, often provide detailed destination guides, insider tips, and firsthand experiences to help you make informed decisions. Gain inspiration, discover hidden gems, and learn valuable insights that will enhance your journey.

Travel guidebooks and websites: Traditional travel guidebooks and official tourism websites are still valuable resources for gathering information about destinations, local attractions, transportation options, cultural experiences, and local customs. Consult trusted travel guidebooks and websites to gather in-depth information about your chosen destinations. Use them as references to create a comprehensive itinerary, immerse yourself in the culture, and explore each location's hidden treasures and beauty.

Local tourism boards and embassies: Visit the official websites of local tourism boards for your chosen destinations. Contact local tourism offices and embassies of your desired destinations for reliable information and assistance. These organizations often can provide comprehensive, up-to-date details on travel regulations and safety advisories. Additionally, they can bring you up to speed on attractions, local events, cultural experiences, and practical details that can enrich your travel experience. Utilize their expertise to ensure a smooth transition and maximize your experience in each location.

Local contacts and cultural ambassadors: Connect with locals and cultural ambassadors who can provide unique insights into your chosen destinations. Engage in conversations, seek their perspectives, and embrace the wisdom they offer. Additionally, leverage your personal network and connections to seek advice and recommendations from individuals who have firsthand knowledge of the destinations you're interested in. Reach out to friends, colleagues, or online acquaintances who may have valuable insights or contacts. By connecting with the people who call these destinations home, you will uncover authentic experiences beyond what guidebooks can provide.

Social media and travel influencers: Follow travel influencers and content creators on social media platforms to discover off-the-beaten-path destinations, hidden gems, and insider tips. Engage with their content, ask questions, and leverage their expertise to refine your travel plans. Social media can be a treasure trove of inspiration and practical advice for your remote work and travel adventure.

Online travel communities, review platforms, and forums: Join online travel communities, forums, and review platforms where experienced travelers and digital nomads share their insights and reviews. Read reviews, ask questions, engage in discussions, and seek recommendations from those who have already explored the destinations you're considering. Embrace the camaraderie of like-minded individuals and find solace in their support and guidance. You will gain a wealth of information about destinations, accommodations, transportation, and more. Connect with other remote workers and travelers through online communities, social media groups, and coworking spaces. Seek recommendations, ask for advice, and tap into their wealth of knowledge and experiences.

Remote work and travel apps: Embrace the power of technology by utilizing remote work resources and travel apps. From booking accommodations and locating reliable Wi-Fi hotspots to finding local transportation options, these digital tools provide convenience and accessibility. Discover platforms that curate authentic experiences and connect you with local communities eager to share their culture with you. These apps can help you find affordable accommodations, connect with local communities, discover co-working spaces, and even manage travel itineraries.

Travel literature and documentaries: Immerse yourself in travel literature and documentaries that capture the essence of various destinations. Allow the written word and visual storytelling to ignite your imagination, giving you glimpses into the cultural tapestry of each place. Discover hidden narratives that inspire and enrich your journey.

Travel planning workshops and seminars: Attend workshops and seminars that specialize in travel planning. Engage with industry experts who can offer valuable insights and tips for optimizing your adventure. Learn about the art of itinerary design, cultural etiquette, and sustainable travel practices. These educational opportunities will equip you with the knowledge and confidence to embark on a transformative journey.

Travel agencies and tour operators: Consider working with reputable travel agencies or tour operators specializing in remote work and travel experiences. These professionals can help streamline your itinerary, provide logistical support, and offer customized packages tailored to your preferences. Leverage their expertise and local connections to create a seamless journey that aligns with your vision.

Evaluate your budget and financial considerations:

It's essential to have a solid grasp of your financial situation when planning your remote work and travel experience. Assess your budget and determine how much you're willing to invest in your journey. Consider accommodation, transportation, meals, activities, and unforeseen expenses. Be resourceful and seek ways to optimize your budget without compromising the quality of your experience. Research cost-of-living information for your chosen destinations and consider ways to minimize costs, such as cooking your meals, using shared workspaces, utilizing travel rewards programs, or exploring affordable accommodation options like homestays or house-sitting. A well-planned budget will allow you to make the most of your adventure, packing it with fulfilling experiences without undue financial stress.

So, pack your bags, charge your devices, and prepare to embark on a journey that will forever reshape your perspective. Cultivate a mindset of openness and curiosity, allowing yourself to be fully present in each moment. The world is waiting to be explored, and with careful planning, a dash of courage, and a thirst for adventure, you will embark on an experience that will create memories that will forever be etched in your heart. Prepare to dive headfirst into a world of wonder where work and play dance harmoniously. Your journey will be a tapestry woven with cultural immersion, self-discovery, and the forging of unforgettable memories.

As you embark on this extraordinary voyage, may your path be filled with awe-inspiring encounters, soul-stirring experiences, and transformative insights. This is your opportunity to expand your horizons, challenge your limitations, and create a truly extraordinary life. As you navigate the intricacies of planning your first remote work adventure, be guided by the principles of perseverance, determination, and unwavering belief in your potential. This is your time to shine, to step out of your comfort zone, and to embrace the exhilaration ahead of you. Stay adaptable and driven, for the adventure of a lifetime awaits you.

Bon voyage, my fellow adventurer! The world awaits, and your remote work adventure is about to take flight. May your travels be filled with unforgettable experiences, unexpected friendships, and a deep sense of fulfillment. The world is calling, and it's time to answer with a resounding "Yes!" Let the adventure begin!

CHAPTER EIGHT

OVERCOMING FEAR AND DOUBT

Making the Leap into a Remote Lifestyle

L et's take a moment to address the fear and resistance that might come up when we start challenging societal norms. The fear of judgment, the fear of failure, and the fear of stepping outside our comfort zones can be real roadblocks. Remember, courage is not the absence of fear; it's taking action despite the presence of fear. It's about embracing vulnerability and being willing to fail forward in pursuit of a life that feels authentic and fulfilling.

To truly empower yourself to embrace the unknown and create a fulfilling and successful remote lifestyle, you need to understand the common fears and doubts that may arise, implement proven techniques to conquer them and cultivate a mindset of confidence and resilience. By tapping into your inner strength, embracing a positive mindset, and building unshakable self-belief, you will unleash your true potential and pave the way for a liberated remote lifestyle filled with success, fulfillment, and adventure. Conquer your fears and write your own success story in the world of remote work and travel. Along the way, we will draw inspiration from the stories and experiences of individuals who have successfully made this leap, proving that the rewards are worth the risks.

Common fears and doubts associated with leaving a stable job for a remote lifestyle

Leaving the security of a stable job to pursue a remote lifestyle can evoke a range of fears and doubts. Let's shed light on some of the most common concerns you may encounter:

Fear of financial instability: When venturing into a remote lifestyle, it's natural to worry about financial stability. The absence of a steady paycheck can be unsettling to most people who have never known any other structure. The prospect of uncertain income and financial stability can be paralyzing. It's natural to worry about the feasibility of sustaining a prosperous lifestyle, remote or otherwise. With resourcefulness and a relentless drive to succeed, you can create multiple income streams and unlock unprecedented financial opportunities. You can create a thriving remote career surpassing a traditional job's financial influx. By developing a comprehensive financial plan, exploring diverse income streams, and embracing a mindset of abundance, you can confidently mitigate these fears and navigate the financial landscape.

Fear of the unknown: The uncertainty that accompanies a new path can be intimidating. The fear of stepping outside your comfort zone and venturing into uncharted territory is natural. However, it's important to remember that growth lies outside your comfort zone. Acknowledge that failure is a natural part of growth and success. Take calculated risks that align with your aspirations and push you closer to your remote lifestyle goals. Also, remember that failure is not permanent unless you allow it to be. Embrace the possibility of setbacks as learning opportunities that will ultimately propel you forward on your journey. Envisage the unknown as an opportunity for self-discovery, learning, and personal growth. Learn from failures, adjust your strategies, and keep moving forward with unwavering determination.

Doubts about professional credibility: When leaving the confines of a traditional office, doubts about professional credibility can creep in. Will others perceive you as competent and dedicated without the corporate facade? Recognizing your unique value and the expertise you bring to the table is crucial. Remember, every successful entrepreneur has faced adversity and navigated uncharted territories. Take inventory of your strengths and identify how they can be leveraged in the remote landscape. By building a robust personal brand, cultivating a reputation for excellence, and continually investing in your professional growth, you can overcome these doubts, showcase your abilities to the world, and establish yourself as an authority in your field.

Fear of isolation and loneliness: The absence of daily face-to-face interactions with colleagues and the routine of an office environment can trigger feelings of isolation and loneliness. However, the digital age has opened up a world of connectivity, and the remote work landscape is brimming with vibrant communities and opportunities for human connection. It's crucial to proactively build a support network of like-minded individuals, whether through remote work communities, co-working spaces, or virtual collaboration.

Embrace digital platforms and participate in networking and remote work events to construct a supportive network that spans across borders and time zones. Seek mentors, join mastermind groups, and engage with fellow remote workers who have successfully made the leap to foster relationships with like-minded individuals who share your passion for exploration. By locking arms with individuals who understand and uplift you, you can build a support network that fuels your growth and brings a sense of camaraderie to your remote journey.

Strategies for overcoming fear and embracing the unknown

Cultivate self-compassion: Acknowledge that fear and doubt are natural responses to change and vulnerability. Treat yourself with kindness and compassion as you navigate this transition. Embrace the mindset that mistakes and setbacks are part of the growth process, and use them as opportunities to learn and improve.

Change your focus and ask empowering questions: Shift your focus from what could go wrong to what could go right. Openly refer to yourself as a "solution finder" instead of a "problem solver." Ask yourself empowering questions that unlock solutions and possibilities. What skills do you possess that are transferable to a remote environment? How can you leverage technology to enhance your productivity and reach? Reframing your mindset and seeking empowering answers will unlock the path to success.

Reframe fear as excitement: Rather than viewing fear as a negative emotion, reframe it as excitement. The physiological responses of fear and excitement are similar, so why not interpret fear as a signal that you are about to embark on something exciting and life-changing? Embrace the rush of anticipation and channel it into fuel for your journey.

Develop a burning desire for your remote lifestyle: Cultivate an unwavering passion for the remote lifestyle you envision. Clearly define your goals, aspirations, and the benefits you seek. Immerse yourself in the vision of your ideal remote lifestyle, and let this drive you forward, overpowering any doubts or fears that may arise.

Take small steps and embrace gradual change: Begin by taking small, manageable steps toward your remote lifestyle. There is something rather cathartic about checking items off your to-do list, so break down your journey into smaller milestones and celebrate each achievement along the way. By embracing gradual change, you consistently and incrementally expand your comfort zone and welcome new experiences.

Research and practice Mel Robbins's 5-Second Rule: When fear and doubt creep in, use the 5-Second Rule. Count backward from 5 and take action. This simple technique interrupts negative thought patterns and propels you into action before fear takes hold. Take that leap of faith, make that crucial phone call, or send that email. Action leads to momentum, and momentum breeds confidence.

Set clear goals and create an action plan: Define your remote lifestyle goals and break them into actionable steps. Create a roadmap that outlines the tasks and milestones you need to achieve along the way. By having a clear plan of action, you can systematically move forward.

Embrace continuous learning and growth: Adopt a growth mindset that celebrates learning, resilience, and adaptability. Commit to a lifelong journey of personal growth. Embrace a curiosity-driven approach to your remote lifestyle, continuously seeking new knowledge and skills that enhance your personal and professional development. Engage in online courses, attend workshops, and participate in industry events that align with your remote work and travel aspirations. The more you invest in yourself, the stronger your confidence will become.

Build a strong foundation of knowledge and preparation: Acquire knowledge and skills relevant to the remote work landscape. Conduct thorough research on remote work opportunities, understand the skills and tools required for success, and invest in continuous learning. Develop a well-rounded skill set that aligns with your remote career goals and positions you as a valuable asset in the digital world.

Gratitude and reflection: Gratitude unlocks a wealth of positivity and abundance. Cultivate a practice of gratitude by reflecting on the opportunities and privileges that a remote lifestyle affords. Instead of focusing on what you don't have in your day-to-day life, focus on what you do and count your blessings accordingly. Embrace a daily gratitude practice to shift your focus toward abundance and possibility. Celebrate small victories and milestones along your journey, reinforcing your confidence in your chosen path.

Positive self-talk: Be mindful of your language when speaking to yourself. Replace self-doubt and negative self-talk with affirmations and empowering statements. Remind yourself of your strengths, accomplishments, and the potential that lies within you. Harness the power of positive self-talk to build resilience and self-assurance.

Stories and experiences of individuals who have successfully made the transition

Drawing inspiration from the stories and experiences of individuals who have successfully transitioned to a remote lifestyle can provide invaluable encouragement. Seek out books, podcasts, and online communities where you can connect with and learn from these trailblazers. Engage in conversations, share your journey, and find solace in the collective wisdom and support of those who have walked a similar path. Their triumphs and challenges will ignite the fire within you and validate your aspirations.

Remember, the path to a remote lifestyle is paved with uncertainty and challenges, and taking the leap requires courage, vulnerability, and a willingness to embrace the unknown. By understanding and addressing your fears and doubts, cultivating a positive mindset, and finding inspiration in the stories of others, you will unlock the transformative power of a remote lifestyle. Embrace the journey with open arms, for it is through facing our fears that we find our truest selves and create a life of purpose and freedom.

CHAPTER NINE

———

BALANCING WORK AND TRAVEL

Maximizing Productivity on the Road

Picture this: you're working on an important project while sipping a coconut on a tropical beach or answering emails from a cozy café in a European city. Sounds like a dream, right? Well, it's not only possible but within your reach. Prepare yourself for an extraordinary adventure where productivity and wanderlust intertwine in perfect synergy. In this fast-paced world of remote work and global exploration, finding the sweet spot of maximized productivity while embracing new experiences on the road is key. Together, we'll uncover the secrets to managing work responsibilities, conquering distractions, and attaining that perfect work-life harmony while exploring the world and avoiding burnout. Get ready to unlock the secrets of being productive and present as you ignite your productivity and supercharge your journey!

Imagine yourself as the architect of your destiny, carefully crafting a blueprint for success. Just as a visionary designer transforms an empty canvas into a work of art, create a detailed plan that outlines your goals and the steps necessary to realize them. Set clear objectives and create a roadmap that will guide you through the twists and turns of your journey. Embrace the power of intention and purpose, for they will guide you through the labyrinth of opportunities that lie ahead. With a well-defined roadmap, you'll navigate the realms of work and travel with clarity and conviction.

Practical tips for managing work responsibilities and eliminating distractions while traveling

Establish your portable office: By leveraging your designated workspace, you create a sacred space wherever you are, a sanctuary where you can immerse yourself in deep work. A space that signals your brain it's time to get in the zone. With your portable command center in place, you can get work done efficiently, amplify your capabilities, and transform your virtual presence into an unstoppable force.

Leverage technology: Just as a skilled craftsman wields the finest instruments, equip yourself with cutting-edge technology. Your trusty laptop becomes an extension of your creative prowess, enabling you to conquer any task that comes your way. Your ability to harness the power of a reliable internet connection is your gateway to the digital realm. Your noise-canceling headphones become the guardians of your aural environment, allowing you to focus fully on the task. Embrace the tranquility of undisturbed workflow, and watch as your productivity soars to unprecedented heights.

Optimize your digital toolbox: Take advantage of technology to streamline your work processes. Utilize productivity apps, project management tools, and communication platforms to stay organized, collaborate with team members, and manage your tasks effectively. Explore time-tracking apps to ensure that you allocate your time wisely and maximize productivity.

Master the art of focus: Distractions are everywhere, especially when exploring new destinations. Remember, focus is a muscle, and the more you flex it, the stronger it becomes, so train yourself to stay laser-focused on your work tasks. Just as a painter loses track of time while lost in their art, find your flow and let your creative genius shine. Leverage the power of focus-related apps to help safeguard your professional playground. Turn off superfluous notifications from the outside world, silence the noise, and unleash your ability to block out distractions, which is a superpower in the digital age.

Plan like a pro: When you're working on the road, it's essential to have a solid plan and organize your work commitments. Think of it like mapping out your adventure route. Set clear objectives, establish deadlines, create a schedule that accommodates your travel plans, and prioritize your tasks like a seasoned explorer navigating uncharted territory. Communicate with your team and clients so everyone is on the same page. With a solid plan in place, you'll be prepared to conquer the work world, no matter where your travels take you.

Strategies for maintaining work-life balance and avoiding burnout

Set boundaries: You're in control of your time, and it's crucial to establish clear boundaries that protect your work and personal life, even while traveling. Communicate your availability to clients, colleagues, and loved ones, and honor those boundaries to maintain a healthy work-life balance. Designate specific working hours and create rituals that signal the start and end of your workday. But also honor your need for rejuvenation and adventure. Give yourself permission to unplug and recharge, guilt-free. Design moments in your schedule to explore new surroundings, embrace the local culture, and recharge your batteries. Remember, you're not just here to work but to live.

Practice self-care: Self-care is not just a luxury—it's a necessity. Prioritize self-care while traveling to avoid burnout. Remember, you can't pour from an empty cup, so take care of yourself first. Just as an athlete nourishes their body with nutrient-rich foods, feed your mind with empowering thoughts and positive affirmations. Think of it as fueling up your tank for the long haul. Engage in activities that rejuvenate your mind, body, and soul. Whether practicing mindfulness, getting some exercise, or indulging in your favorite hobbies, make self-care a non-negotiable part of your routine. You'll be amazed at how it boosts your energy and enhances your productivity and overall well-being. Your well-being is the foundation upon which your success is built.

Embrace flexibility: Take advantage of your location independence to schedule work around your travel experiences. Adapt and pivot, finding the perfect balance between work and adventure. Remember, life is an ever-changing landscape, and you're the artist painting your masterpiece. Be flexible in your plans, for it is often in the spontaneous detours that the most remarkable adventures await. Allow yourself to explore new destinations, immerse in local culture, and indulge in enriching experiences. By embracing flexibility, you can find harmony between work and travel, enhancing both aspects of your journey.

Finding the synergy between productivity and presence

Achieving the perfect balance between productivity and presence is an art form. Here are some powerful practices to embrace:

Cultivate mindfulness: Stay present in each moment of your daily activities, whether you're working on a project, exploring a new destination, or savoring the flavors of foreign cuisines. Practice mindfulness by fully immersing yourself in the experience at hand. When you work, give it your undivided attention. When you explore, be fully present and absorb the richness of your surroundings. This balance allows you to excel both professionally and personally.

Prioritize meaningful experiences: Focus on quality rather than quantity when it comes to both work and travel. Instead of rushing through a checklist of tourist attractions, seek out experiences that align with your passions and values. Aim for depth rather than breadth. Apply the same principle to your work—prioritize meaningful tasks that contribute to your long-term goals, focusing on accomplishing impactful work rather than getting caught up in busywork. You create a life of purpose and fulfillment by prioritizing quality over quantity.

Reflect and refine: Take the time to reflect on your work and travel experiences regularly. Evaluate what's working and what needs adjustment. Celebrate your wins, learn from your challenges, and make necessary refinements to optimize your productivity and well-being. By remaining open to growth and being willing to make necessary changes, you can continuously refine your balance between productivity and presence. Remember, growth is a continuous process, and the path to success is paved with intentional reflection and refinement.

As we conclude this chapter, remember that balancing work and travel is an art form, and you are the artist. Embrace the beauty of each moment, whether you're conquering a work deadline or immersing yourself in a new culture. Find joy in the journey and let the experiences you encounter shape and inspire your work. By implementing the practical tips and strategies in this chapter, you can navigate the challenges, maximize productivity, and cultivate a sense of fulfillment in your remote work and travel lifestyle. With every step, you grow closer to achieving the extraordinary life you envision. Remember, this is your opportunity to create a fulfilling and adventurous life.

CHAPTER TEN

———

DIGITAL NOMAD HACKS

Tips and Tricks for Seamless Travel and Work Integration

Welcome to the exhilarating realm of digital nomadism, where the world becomes your playground, your office is wherever you choose it to be, and boundless horizons await. We're talking about the ultimate fusion of work and travel, where you can navigate the globe and make a living simultaneously.

Together, we will delve into the practical strategies and actionable tips that will elevate your digital nomad game. Along the way, we will uncover a wealth of strategies, hacks, and tactics to enhance your journey as a digital nomad. So, grab your metaphorical passport and join me as we embark on a transformative exploration of the digital nomad lifestyle that's equal parts adventure and accomplishment.

Packing essentials for digital nomads: what to bring and what to leave behind

Imagine yourself standing at the precipice of an incredible adventure with a single suitcase as your gateway to the world. Picture yourself as a master packer, skillfully selecting the essentials that will accompany you on your nomadic adventures. As you prepare for your journey, it's crucial to pack wisely, selecting items that align with your nomadic lifestyle and optimize your efficiency. Just as a skilled strategist picks the most valuable tools for their mission, you too, must curate your travel arsenal thoughtfully and with intention. Take a moment to pause and reflect on what truly serves you on this journey.

Start by creating a comprehensive packing list, including a reliable laptop, universal power adapters, noise-canceling headphones, and a comfortable backpack. Consider your work requirements and the destinations you'll explore, then pack accordingly. Opt for lightweight, multi-functional items that serve multiple purposes and adapt to various climates. Seek out versatile clothing and accessories that can be mixed and matched effortlessly, like a Swiss Army knife of productivity, allowing you to transition between work and play seamlessly. Embrace the art of minimalism, leaving behind unnecessary baggage and embracing the freedom of mobility. Remember, the key to successful packing is striking a balance between practicality and resourcefulness, and the true value lies not in the quantity but in the quality and functionality of the items you carry. When it comes to packing, less is more, so the lighter your load, the freer your spirit.

Strategies for finding suitable accommodations for remote work

As a digital nomad, your accommodation becomes a sanctuary where work and rest intertwine. Your choice of accommodations can make or break your digital nomad experience. Finding the perfect spot to set up your digital nomad HQ is crucial for maintaining a productive and fulfilling lifestyle on the road. Seek spaces that offer comfort, functionality, and a conducive work environment while providing opportunities to connect with the local culture and community. Whether it's a cozy apartment in a vibrant city or a picturesque retreat surrounded by nature's splendor, find your sanctuary where productivity and inspiration coexist in perfect harmony.

Carefully weigh factors such as location, amenities, the availability of a dedicated workspace, and infrastructure and community when selecting your temporary home. Research co-living spaces or apartments that cater to the needs of digital nomads. These spaces often provide amenities like high-speed internet, comfortable work areas, a vibrant atmosphere, and opportunities for networking and collaboration with like-minded individuals. Embrace the power of community, as it can provide support, inspiration, and collaboration on your journey. Actively explore the diversity of your surroundings, immersing yourself in the local culture and drawing inspiration from new perspectives. Allow each destination to inspire and fuel your creative endeavors. Remember, the world is your stage, and your choice of accommodation is the backdrop against which your extraordinary life unfolds.

Staying connected on the road: managing internet access and data plans

In the digital age, connectivity is the lifeblood that sustains our nomadic ambitions. Your digital presence becomes the bridge between your dreams and reality. It's your lifeline to clients, colleagues, and the world at large. To ensure seamless communication and productivity, it's essential to have a solid plan in place to ensure reliable internet access and data plans, ensuring a smooth flow of connectivity wherever your nomadic path takes you.

Explore local SIM cards or portable Wi-Fi devices that offer reliable connectivity across borders. Explore co-working spaces, cafes, or libraries that provide a productive work environment with stable connectivity for your work sessions. Embrace the art of adaptability, for each destination brings its unique network landscape. With a reliable connection, you can find innovative ways to stay connected and seamlessly bridge the gap between work and wanderlust.

Additionally, consider investing in a virtual private network (VPN) to enhance security while accessing public networks. Also, use cloud-based storage solutions to access your files from anywhere and maintain seamless collaboration with clients and colleagues. By staying proactive and resourceful, you'll conquer any connectivity challenges that come your way.

Tools and apps for managing travel logistics, finances, and communications

Now, let's discuss the tools that will make your nomadic life a breeze. As a modern nomad, your digital toolkit becomes an indispensable companion. Discover travel apps that offer real-time flight updates, accommodation booking platforms that cater to your preferences, and transportation apps that make navigating unfamiliar territories a breeze. Focus on travel apps that unlock the door to seamless itinerary planning, providing real-time updates and personalized recommendations. Embrace communication tools that bridge the distance between you and your clients, colleagues, and loved ones, fostering meaningful connections despite the physical miles. In the next chapter, we will also explore finance apps that track your expenses effortlessly, allowing you to maintain financial stability and make informed decisions. Remember, your digital toolkit is a testament to your resourcefulness and adaptability. Let technology guide you as you navigate the vast horizons of remote work and travel.

Below are some tools and digital resources that will empower you to navigate the nomadic lifestyle with confidence, efficiency, and charm. With a vast array of apps and tools at your disposal on this journey, we will focus on four main categories: Travel, Project Management, Time Management/Organization, and Lifestyle. Remember, these tools are just a means to an end and only a meager selection of available resources in the ever-evolving digital landscape. From productivity to communication and everything in between, the proper tools will make your nomadic journey smoother, more efficient, and a lot of fun. Choosing the ones that align with your specific needs and work style is important. Experiment, iterate, and find the perfect combination that empowers you to thrive along your journey. They are listed below in roughly alphabetical order, with a few similar tools and resources grouped together for efficiency purposes. So, dive right in and uncover the immense value they offer!

Travel apps

Airbnb/Agoda/HomeAway/VRBO: When finding unique accommodations during your travels, vacation rentals are the digital nomad's best friend. It offers a wide range of rentals, from cozy apartments to luxurious villas, allowing you to live like a local wherever you go. Say goodbye to mundane hotels and embrace unforgettable nomadic adventures. There is also a wide variety of vacation rental platforms that cater specifically to the digital nomad and focus on amenities geared toward making the work-travel life seamless.

Google Maps: Navigation is made simple with Google Maps. Whether you're exploring a new city or searching for a hidden gem, this app provides detailed directions, real-time traffic updates, and public transportation information. It even allows you to save maps offline for your planned destinations so you can still access directions even when offline. Additionally, it lets you track your adventures as you go along so you can go back and view your travel history to put pins in the globe digitally.

Google Translate: Break down language barriers and

communicate with locals using Google Translate. This handy tool can translate text, speech, and even signs, making it a valuable asset in your global travels. Now, you can immerse yourself in new cultures and connect with people effortlessly in real-time.

Nomad List: Discovering the best destinations for digital nomads becomes effortless with Nomad List. This platform provides valuable information on the cost of living, internet speed, safety, and more, empowering you to choose your next adventure wisely. Make informed decisions as you explore new horizons.

Skyscanner/Google Flights/Kayak: Find the best deals on flights, hotels, and car rentals. These search platforms compare prices from various travel providers and dates. Feeling more adventurous and wanting to leave your next adventure to chance? Use the "Explore" feature to discover exciting destinations within your budget. It's like spinning a globe and letting fate guide you to your next epic work-travel destination. Picture this: you find a great flight deal, but you're not ready to book just yet. No worries! With these search tools, you can track the prices of specific flights and routes. You'll get notified of price changes, ensuring you never miss out on those sweet deals. This means you can easily adjust your travel plans to snag those budget-friendly flights, ensuring you get the most bang for your buck.

TripIt: Organize your travel itineraries and stay on top of your adventures with TripIt. This handy app creates a master trip itinerary, allowing you to consolidate flight details, accommodation information, and activities in one place. Access your travel plans anytime, anywhere, and embark on your journeys stress-free.

Work Project/Product Management apps

Asana: Asana is a project management tool that enables you to assign tasks, set deadlines, and track progress with team members. Plan, organize, and track your projects with this versatile tool. Asana helps you streamline your workflow, assign tasks, and collaborate seamlessly with your team. Foster collaboration, streamline workflows, and bring your vision to life.

Canva: Visual content has the power to captivate and engage, and Canva makes it easy to create professional designs even without graphic design skills. From social media posts to presentations, this user-friendly tool offers a wide range of templates and customization options, enabling you to visually express your ideas and leave a lasting impression. Let your creativity shine and leave a lasting impression.

Grammarly: In the pursuit of excellence, effective communication is paramount. Elevate your writing to new heights with Grammarly. This digital writing assistant acts as your grammar guru, providing real-time suggestions and ensuring your messages, emails, and documents are clear, concise, polished, and error-free. Enhance your writing skills and leave a lasting impression with every word.

LastPass: Security is a top priority in our interconnected world, and LastPass simplifies password management and enhances online security. Safeguard your digital assets and protect sensitive information with this robust password manager. Enjoy peace of mind and focus on what truly matters, knowing your online presence is protected.

LinkedIn: Networking is a cornerstone of success, and LinkedIn provides the ultimate platform for professional connections. Build your brand, showcase your expertise, and connect with like-minded individuals who can propel your career forward. Unlock the potential of networking and open doors to new opportunities. LinkedIn Sales Navigator allows entrepreneurs and sales professionals to identify and connect with potential clients, which is crucial. This comprehensive tool on the platform provides advanced search capabilities, lead recommendations, and insights to help you navigate the realm of B2B sales.

Slack: Effective communication and collaboration are crucial for success, and Slack is a messaging app that brings all your conversations, files, and tools into one place, ensuring seamless communication. Create channels, join discussions, and stay connected with your team, no matter where you are in the world. Foster collaboration and achieve extraordinary results.

Todoist/Wunderlist: Stay organized and conquer your to-do list with Todoist. This powerful task management tool allows you to create, prioritize, and track tasks across devices. With its intuitive interface and smart features, you'll stay focused, meet deadlines, and easily achieve your goals.

Trello: With Trello, you can effortlessly organize your projects using visual boards, lists, and cards. It's like having a virtual whiteboard where you can easily track tasks, set deadlines, and collaborate. This tool helps you stay focused, prioritize your work, and clearly achieve your goals.

VPN (Virtual Private Network): Protecting your online privacy is paramount, and a VPN ensures your digital footprint remains secure. This powerful tool encrypts your internet connection, allowing you to browse the web anonymously and access geo-restricted content. Safeguard your online presence while exploring the digital realm, even on public Wi-Fi.

Zapier: Automation is a key component of productivity, and Zapier allows you to connect your favorite apps and automate repetitive tasks. Create custom workflows, integrate different tools, and save valuable time and energy. Unleash the power of automation and optimize your workflow.

Zoom: When face-to-face interaction is key, Zoom is your go-to tool. Whether hosting virtual meetings, conducting webinars, or catching up with loved ones, Zoom enables you to connect authentically. It's a powerful tool that bridges distances and fosters meaningful connections in the digital realm.

ZoomShift: Managing a remote team's schedules and shifts can be challenging, but ZoomShift simplifies the process. This employee scheduling software enables you to create schedules, track attendance, and communicate with your team effortlessly, ensuring everyone is on the same page. Streamline your operations and ensure smooth coordination. With its intuitive interface and automated features, you'll streamline your team's workflow, enhancing productivity and harmony.

Work Time Management and Organization apps

Calendly: Simplify scheduling and save precious time with Calendly. This invaluable tool lets you share your availability, allowing others to book meetings and calls that seamlessly align with your calendar. Say goodbye to the hassle of back-and-forth emails and embrace efficiency. Calendly allows you to book time slots that work for both parties.

Dropbox/Google Drive: Effortlessly store, share, and access your files from anywhere with cloud storage platforms. These tools ensure that your important documents, photos, and videos are safely backed up and readily available, even when you're on the move. Embrace the convenience of cloud storage, digital file storage, and collaboration in real-time to streamline efficiency.

Evernote: Napoleon Hill believed in the power of capturing ideas, and Evernote serves as the modern-day equivalent of a mastermind notebook. With this digital tool, you can jot down your thoughts, record voice memos, save articles, and organize your research in one convenient place. With its synchronization across devices, you can access your ideas anytime, anywhere, ensuring you never miss a brilliant insight. Harness the power of your ideas and turn them into actionable plans.

Focus@Will: To achieve greatness, concentration is essential, and Focus@Will provides the perfect backdrop for deep work. This music streaming service curates scientifically optimized playlists to enhance focus and productivity. Let the power of music propel you toward your goals.

Forest: Distraction is the enemy of progress, and focused work is the key to digital nomad success. Forest is a unique app that helps you stay on track by gamifying productivity. Plant a virtual tree and watch it grow as you resist the temptation to use your phone. Cultivate your focus and create a forest of achievements.

Harvest: Accurately tracking your time and managing projects is essential as a digital nomad, and Harvest delivers precisely that. This time tracking and invoicing tool helps you monitor your work hours, generate professional invoices, and gain insights into your productivity. Efficiently manage your time while staying on top of your earnings.

RescueTime: Time management is a key principle for digital nomad success, and RescueTime allows you to master this aspect of your life. This tool tracks how you spend time on various applications and websites, providing insightful reports that help you make informed decisions about your daily habits. Take control of your time and make every moment count.

Timezone.io/World Time Buddy: Mastering time zones becomes effortless with these time zone tracking apps. As a digital nomad, you'll navigate different time zones regularly, and these tools keep you in sync. With a glance, you'll know the current time in multiple locations, allowing you to schedule meetings easily.

Toggl: Time is a valuable resource, and Toggl helps you track and manage it effectively. This time-tracking tool allows you to measure the time you spend on different tasks and projects, providing valuable insights for optimizing your productivity. Take control of your time and make every minute count.

Lifestyle apps

Buffer/Hootsuite: Consistent social media presence is essential in today's digital landscape and leverages the power of effective self-promotion. Buffer and Hootsuite simplify social media management, allowing you to schedule and automate your posts across different platforms at optimal times, analyze their performance, and grow your online following. These tools will enable you to maintain an active and consistent online presence even when you're off the grid. Build your online presence and amplify your message to the world.

Calm/Headspace: The significance of mental and emotional well-being in achieving success is immeasurable. Meditation and relaxation apps help you find inner peace, reduce stress, and boost your productivity. Take a few moments daily to quiet your mind and unleash your full potential.

Duolingo: Learning the local language adds a delightful layer to your nomadic journey. This language learning platform gamifies the process, allowing you to learn a new language or brush up on your language skills, making it fun and engaging wherever you are. Embrace the power of communication and make deeper connections wherever you roam.

Pocket: Continuous learning helps you remain engaged and grow while on the go. Pocket provides a platform for saving and organizing articles, videos, and web pages for later consumption. Curate your digital library, expand your knowledge, and stay inspired wherever you go. The ability to sync across devices allows you to curate your own digital library for those moments of inspiration.

As we conclude this chapter, remember that the digital nomad lifestyle is not just about work and travel—it's about embracing freedom, exploration, and personal growth, ever perfecting the art of seamless travel and work integration, harnessing the power of technology, resourcefulness, and financial acumen to immerse yourself in the countless cultures and experiences that await you. Let the world become your playground, and your work becomes an expression of your passions and purpose. By optimizing your packing, finding suitable accommodations, staying connected, and utilizing the right tools and apps, you create a solid foundation for a fulfilling and seamless work and travel integration. The possibilities are boundless, and as a digital nomad, you have the power to create a life of freedom, fulfillment, and endless exploration.

CHAPTER ELEVEN

NAVIGATING FINANCES

Budgeting, Taxes, and Financial Independence

A midst the exhilaration of your digital nomad lifestyle, financial stability becomes the bedrock of your journey. As wise investors diversify their portfolios, cultivate financial discipline and savvy money management skills. Explore banking options that offer flexibility and accessibility, such as online banking and digital payment platforms. Create a budget that accounts for your work and travel expenses, allowing you to make informed choices that align with your long-term goals. With financial freedom, you can unlock the full potential of your nomadic adventure.

Once you have a clear picture of your income and expenses, structure realistic financial plans. What are you saving for? A dream trip to Bali or building an emergency fund? Be intentional and prioritize your financial well-being. And here's a pro tip: automate your savings. Set up automatic transfers to a separate savings account so you're consistently putting money aside. It's like magic.

You can automate your funds to be disbursed between different types of accounts that all build toward other dreams and financial goals.

Establishing a budget for a remote work and travel lifestyle

Budgeting is the backbone of financial success. It's all about knowing where your hard-earned dollars are going and making intentional choices. Start by assessing your income and expenses and set clear financial plans that align with your dreams and aspirations.

Spend your money on purpose and with clarity that leaves no room for confusion. Imagine describing your financial plans to a bright seven-year-old. Break it down and map it out clearly.

What are your fixed costs, like accommodations, utilities, and insurance?

How much do you spend on transportation, food, and entertainment?

Identify those discretionary expenses that bring you joy and don't forget to factor in those unexpected expenses that life likes to throw at you.

Also, keep an eye on your spending patterns. Are you indulging in too many lattes or treating yourself to that extra pair of shoes? Remember, it's all about conscious choices. But a budget is not merely about cutting back and restriction; it's about empowerment. It's about aligning your spending habits with your aspirations.

Clearly define your financial objectives, whether building an emergency fund, investing in your future, or embarking on thrilling globetrotting adventures. Then, allocate your resources accordingly. Get crystal clear on your numbers and create a budget that keeps you on track while allowing you to thrive in your adventure lifestyle.

Strategies for tracking expenses and managing finances while on the road

When you're out exploring the world, tracking expenses can feel like herding cats, but it is completely manageable with effective tools and rock-solid financial plans. Embrace the power of technology and get some intuitive apps to help you stay organized, monitor your spending, and ensure you don't blow your budget on that extra guacamole.

There are fantastic apps out there that make expense tracking a breeze. Find one that suits your style, and let it be your trusty sidekick on this financial journey. A couple of examples that you may find useful are as follows:

Expensify: Say goodbye to the headache of managing receipts and expense reports with Expensify. This handy tool streamlines the process, enabling you to effortlessly capture receipts, categorize expenses, and generate comprehensive reports. Now, you can spend more time exploring and less time buried in paperwork.

Xero: Keeping your finances in order is vital for any digital nomad, and Xero simplifies the task. This cloud-based accounting software empowers you to track expenses, manage invoices, and gain valuable insights into your financial health. Stay on top of your finances while focusing on your adventures.

TransferWise: Managing finances across borders is seamless with TransferWise. This trusted platform enables you to easily send and receive money internationally and at low fees. TransferWise offers fast and secure transfers, ensuring you can manage your finances hassle-free. Say goodbye to expensive bank transfers and enjoy hassle-free financial transactions as you navigate the globe.

But tracking expenses is just the first step. It's important to review and analyze your spending regularly. Are there any areas where you can cut back? Are you overspending in certain categories? Look for patterns and make adjustments as needed. Remember, every dollar counts. It's not about being a penny-pincher; it's about being mindful. Treat your finances like a game and make it fun. Set spending limits, challenge yourself to find creative ways to save, and always monitor your financial health. Your future self will thank you.

Understanding tax implications and seeking professional advice where needed

Ah, taxes. They're about as fun as a root canal but a necessary part of adulting. As a digital nomad, you may encounter some unique tax situations. Different countries, different rules. It can get complicated. So, arm yourself with knowledge and align yourself with trusted professionals to guide you. It's crucial to understand the tax implications of your newfound freedom. Educate yourself on the tax laws of your home country and any potential obligations that may arise while working and living abroad. Consult with a tax professional specializing in international taxation to ensure compliance and optimize your tax strategy.

The labyrinth of taxes can become too perplexing to traverse alone. Seek out professional advice and services from licensed and accredited professionals. Enlist the aid of tax advisors who specialize in cross-border taxation. They possess the expertise to guide you through the intricate maze of tax compliance, ensuring you navigate the fiscal landscape confidently and easily. A good accountant or CPA (certified public accountant) can be your financial guru, guiding you through the murky waters of tax regulations and helping you optimize your financial strategy. Remember, it's all about staying compliant and maximizing your money management. Research, ask questions, and consult with professionals where needed. Trust me, it's worth the investment.

Building financial independence and creating multiple income streams

Financial independence is the ultimate destination. It's the holy grail of freedom that allows you to create a life where you forge your path toward lasting prosperity. A life that thrives on the flexibility to make choices without being limited by monetary concerns and constraints. It's time to free yourself of financial stress and create a life of abundance.

The key is to think beyond the paycheck and explore various ways to diversify your income streams. To achieve this, it's important to think beyond a single source of income. Explore opportunities to diversify your earnings and create multiple income streams. Look for opportunities to create passive income streams, such as investing in income automation opportunities, real estate investing, or starting an online business. The more income streams you have, the more secure your financial future becomes.

Think beyond the traditional 9-to-5 grind. Explore and monetize your passions, leveraging your unique skills and expertise. Is there a side hustle you can start? Can you monetize your hobbies or turn your knowledge into a profitable venture? Let your creative genius run wild as you discover new avenues to generate wealth and unlock the gates to financial independence. Can you create an online course or launch a digital product? How about investing in real estate or starting a profitable blog? Educate yourself about different investment options and seek advice from experts. Building wealth takes time and effort, so be patient and stay focused on your long-term vision. The world is your oyster, so don't settle for mediocrity when greatness awaits. The possibilities are endless.

Tap into your skills and passions. Consider freelancing, consulting, or starting a side hustle. Invest in yourself by learning new skills that can open doors to additional income opportunities. Embrace the digital world and explore online businesses, e-commerce, or digital product creation. The opportunities are myriad. It's time to unleash your inner entrepreneur. Develop online courses and programs that you can create once and sell online over and over again to create residual revenue streams—hedge against relying on trading time for money as much as possible. Construct multiple streams of income that can work for you while you sleep so you can reduce financial stress and improve your financial and overall well-being.

Remember, building financial independence takes time and effort. It requires discipline and patience. It's not an overnight transformation. Stay committed to your plans, educate yourself about investment opportunities, cultivate a mindset of continuous learning, and be willing to take calculated risks. Your financial future is waiting for you to claim it. Be patient, stay focused, and celebrate every small win along the way. Your journey toward lasting prosperity begins now.

So, my fellow adventurers, embrace the world of finances with open arms. Budget like a boss, track your expenses like a digital detective, understand tax obligations like a masterful genius, and build your fortress of financial independence like a champion. It's not always easy, but it's worth it. Your financial well-being is an integral part of your overall journey. The path may be challenging, but the rewards are immeasurable. So conquer the financial frontier and create a life of abundance and freedom.

CHAPTER TWELVE

OVERCOMING OBSTACLES

Dealing with Challenges and Setback on Your Journey

Welcome to the heart of the matter– those pesky hurdles and setbacks that remote workers and travelers often encounter on their journey. While it may seem like a dream to work and travel simultaneously, it's not without its fair share of obstacles. It's important to acknowledge that no path is without obstacles, but how we navigate them truly defines our success. So, let's explore how to turn challenges into opportunities, build resilience, and emerge even stronger on your nomadic journey, allowing you to adapt and thrive in the face of adversity.

One of the most common challenges for remote workers is cultivating and maintaining a healthy work-life harmony. When your work and personal life blend together, setting boundaries and prioritizing self-care can be challenging. We'll discuss practical tips for creating a structure that supports your professional and personal well-being, ensuring you can be fully present in both areas of your life.

Embracing the Power of Persistence: When life throws you a curveball, it's essential to adopt a tenacious spirit. Embrace the power of persistence by staying determined and refusing to give up. Instead, channel your inner warrior and keep pushing forward. Remember, setbacks aren't game-enders; they're merely detours on the road to success. Lean into them, learn from their lessons, and let them fuel your determination.

Another obstacle many face is the feeling of isolation or lack of connection. Being away from traditional office environments and coworkers can sometimes leave us craving social interaction. We'll explore ways to proactively build a sense of community, whether it's through joining remote work groups, attending coworking events, or leveraging technology to connect with like-minded individuals.

Practicing Resilience: Resilience is the ability to bounce back from setbacks and keep moving forward. Of course, unexpected situations and unforeseen challenges are bound to arise while on the road. It could be a travel delay, a sudden change in plans, or even a technical glitch that disrupts your workflow. Adaptability is a crucial skill for navigating the nomadic lifestyle. Develop resilience by consistently taking action, focusing on your strengths, reframing challenges as opportunities for growth, and persisting even when faced with adversity. Analyze the situation, extract valuable lessons, and apply them to future endeavors. Reframing setbacks as valuable experiences will give you wisdom and insights that propel you further on your nomadic journey.

Like a chameleon blending into its environment, learn to adapt to changing circumstances. Roll with the proverbial punches. Be flexible and open-minded, ready to shift gears when the situation demands it. Those who can adapt quickly are the ones who thrive. Equip yourself with strategies for adapting and problem-solving in these situations, helping you stay calm and focused even when things don't go according to plan. This flexibility will not only help you overcome setbacks but also allow you to experience the beauty of spontaneity and new opportunities.

Activate Your Winning Mindset: Listen up because this one's a game-changer. Your mindset can either make or break your journey. So, get your mental game on point. Cultivate a success mindset by believing in your abilities and visualizing your desired outcomes. Replace self-doubt with self-confidence and negative thoughts with positive affirmations. Your mind is a powerful tool that shapes your reality and propels you toward success. You're capable of greatness, and it's time to unleash your full potential. Positive thoughts, positive actions, positive results – that's the name of the game.

Building a Supportive Network: No one conquers challenges alone. Having a supportive network is crucial when dealing with challenges on the road. Join online communities, attend meetups, or connect with fellow travelers in co-working spaces. Build strong relationships with like-minded individuals who uplift and support you, even if they are not physically in the same geographic location as you. Actively network with people who understand the unique challenges of the nomadic lifestyle. Talk with them openly about the challenges you're facing. Collaboration and sharing wisdom is where the magic happens. You never know when they may have overcome similar hurdles and can offer practical advice when needed.

Seeking Guidance and Mentorship: Sometimes, challenges may feel overwhelming, and it's important to seek support when needed. You don't have to figure it all out alone, my friend. There are mentors and guides who've walked the path before you. Don't be afraid to ask for help and soak up their wisdom. Their advice, knowledge, and support will light your way. Their insight can provide a fresh perspective, help you navigate challenges with greater ease, and make the journey smoother. Also, don't hesitate to contact professionals, such as therapists, who can guide and help you navigate tough times. Seeking support is a sign of strength and can make a significant difference in your ability to overcome challenges. Remember, the road to success is seldom traveled alone, and success is sweeter when shared.

Cultivating Self-Compassion: Self-compassion is vital when facing setbacks. Treat yourself with kindness and understanding. Remember that setbacks and missteps are a natural part of any journey, and they don't define your worth or potential. Instead of berating yourself for mistakes, practice self-compassion and use your bounce-back ability to set you apart. With unwavering resilience and self-compassion, you'll weather any storm that comes your way.

Prioritizing Self-Care: Self-care is crucial for maintaining physical, emotional, and mental well-being on your nomadic journey. Set aside time for activities that recharge and nourish you. Whether it's practicing mindfulness, engaging in physical exercise, or indulging in hobbies, prioritize self-care to ensure you have the energy and resilience to face challenges head-on.

Embracing Vulnerability: One of the first steps in overcoming challenges is acknowledging and embracing vulnerability. Recognize that it's okay to feel uncertain or anxious about the unknown. Allowing yourself to be vulnerable opens the door to growth and resilience. Share your experiences and challenges with fellow nomads or supportive communities, creating connections and finding strength in shared experiences.

Remember, the nomadic lifestyle is an adventure filled with incredible experiences, personal growth, and new horizons. Embracing vulnerability, practicing self-compassion, and building resilience will empower you to face any challenge that may come your way. By proactively addressing common obstacles, developing resilience, consistently embracing a positive mindset, staying adaptable, and fostering a supportive network, you'll not only overcome obstacles but also thrive in the nomadic lifestyle, creating a life that is truly fulfilling and authentic to you.

CHAPTER THIRTEEN

———

CHOOSING YOUR DESTINATIONS

Unveiling the World's Remote Work Hotspots

As you continue your journey, the travel bug will begin to bite, and the realm of possibilities is virtually endless. Let's explore the factors to consider when choosing remote work destinations, highlight some of the most sought-after locations, and equip you with practical tips to make the best decision for your nomadic journey. From bustling cities to tranquil beaches, we'll dig into the elements to consider when selecting your desired destinations, the vibrant digital nomad communities, and the unforgettable experiences awaiting you.

Follow Your Inner Compass: When choosing a remote work destination, it's crucial to align your location with your passions and interests. Picture this: waking up daily in a place that fuels your fire and ignites your passion. Listen to that voice inside you, urging you to explore new horizons and indulge your passions. Take a moment to reflect on what truly energizes and inspires you. You'll set the stage for a fulfilling and purpose-driven nomadic experience by aligning your destination with your passions.

Research Like a Pro: When it comes to finding your remote work utopia, knowledge is your secret weapon. Learn about the local culture, safety, and infrastructure of potential destinations. Seek out reliable sources, read travel blogs, and connect with fellow nomads who have experienced these locations firsthand. Engage with them and inquire about their real-life experiences to gather insights and insider tips. The more you know, the more confident and empowered you'll be in making the right choice. This diligent research will arm you with invaluable insights, enabling you to make informed decisions about the destinations that align with your lifestyle and aspirations.

Consider the Practicalities: While adventure and excitement are essential, it's also crucial to consider the practicalities of remote work destinations. Research the cost of living, local amenities, healthcare facilities, and transportation options to ensure a smooth transition. By being practical in your choices, you set yourself up for a fulfilling and sustainable remote work lifestyle.

Safety First: Let's talk about safety. Your well-being is paramount, so choosing destinations with a good safety track record is important. Research the local crime rates, political stability, and healthcare infrastructure of your potential destinations. It's all about finding that sweet spot where you can explore and work with peace of mind.

The Nomad Network: Arguably, the thriving digital nomad community is one of the most incredible aspects of the nomadic lifestyle. Picture this: like-minded individuals from all corners of the globe coming together to support, connect, and collaborate. Seek destinations with established nomad networks, co-working spaces, and meet-up events. Remember, when you surround yourself with like-minded individuals, you create a support system that will propel you towards your goals. The connections you make and the friendships you form will enrich your journey beyond measure.

Unforgettable Experiences: As a nomad, you have the unique opportunity to immerse yourself in the cultures, traditions, and wonders of each destination. Embrace new experiences, try exotic cuisines, learn the local customs, and explore the hidden gems of each region. Whether it's hiking to majestic waterfalls, meditating in ancient temples, or dancing the night away at vibrant festivals, the world is your playground, and adventure awaits at every turn.

Nomad-friendly Infrastructure: As a modern nomad, you need infrastructure to thrive - comfortable workspaces that can keep up with your adventurous spirit. Seek out destinations that cater to your remote work needs, offering reliable internet connectivity, co-working spaces, and amenities designed with the wandering spirit in mind. Find places you can effortlessly connect with like-minded individuals, collaborate on exciting projects, and create lifelong friendships. A robust infrastructure will be your compass, guiding you towards productivity and success. Access to a supportive network and reliable technology will be your foundation for success and endless possibilities.

Harmony of Work and Play: Let's face it: remote work is about more than just work. It's about creating a life that blends productivity with adventure. While remote work is a wonderful opportunity to explore the world, it still requires dedication and discipline. Look for destinations that offer a harmonious balance between work and play. Find places where you can explore breathtaking landscapes, engage in thrilling activities, and rejuvenate your spirit during your downtime. Prioritize your self-care and create boundaries to ensure you don't burn out. A healthy work-life integration will empower you to fully embrace the nomadic lifestyle and maximize your experiences.

Embrace Cultural Immersion: The world is a vibrant tapestry of diverse cultures, languages, and customs. Picture yourself walking the streets of a foreign land, immersing yourself in the myriad experiences it brings. Embrace the beauty of diversity as you choose a remote work destination. Seek places where diverse traditions and customs converge, where every corner reveals a new facet of humanity. Engage with local communities, participate in traditional festivals, and explore each place's unique offerings. By immersing yourself in different cultures, you'll expand your horizons, gain new perspectives, and foster empathy for different ways of life.

Armed with your inner compass, a solid research foundation,

an appreciation for diverse cultures, a robust infrastructure, and a commitment to work-play integration, you're ready to chart your course to the ultimate remote work destination. Believe in yourself, follow your dreams, embrace the adventure, and let the world unfold its wonders as you carve your path to greatness. The world is calling, and it's time to answer, so let's explore a few destinations that check the boxes as cultural hubs for digital nomads:

Bali, Indonesia - The Tropical Paradise

Let's launch our digital nomad tour in Bali, where lush rice terraces and waterfalls meet stunning beaches. Bali's not just about picturesque landscapes, coconuts, and surfboards; it's got a thriving digital nomad scene that makes it a digital nomad's dream. The island offers a plethora of co-working spaces tucked away in vibrant jungle settings and bustling beach towns like Hubud and Dojo Bali. The cost of living here is a steal, making it a haven for budget-savvy nomads who enjoy indulging in delicious local cuisine without breaking the bank. Their digital nomad visa is an excellent way to explore the country for a very lengthy period without having to renew your visa. The Wi-Fi is generally reliable, although it can get a bit shaky during Bali's rainy season. Plus, Bali's nomad community is exceptionally welcoming, making it easy to find like-minded individuals to connect and collaborate with; you'll be trading your cubicle for a hammock in no time.

Chiang Mai, Thailand - The Cultural Hub

Next stop, Chiang Mai, Thailand - a vibrant city that is famous for its affordability and rich cultural experiences. It beautifully blends ancient temples with modern amenities. The cost of living here is unbelievably low, and you'll be like a kid in a candy store when it comes to delectable street food. The digital nomad community here is well-established, with regular meet-up events and workshops. Co-working spaces like Punspace and CAMP provide reliable internet and a productive atmosphere. The laid-back vibe and countless cultural experiences make Chiang Mai a top pick. Explore historic temples, venture into the jungle, or simply enjoy a Thai massage - Chiang Mai has it all.

Medellín, Colombia - The City of Eternal Spring

Now, let's salsa our way to Medellín, Colombia. Known as the "City of Eternal Spring" for its perfect weather, this place offers an irresistible mix of affordability and innovation. The city boasts modern co-working spaces like Selina and AtomHouse, which offer excellent facilities with robust Wi-Fi coverage. Nomads flock here for its friendly locals and the opportunity to explore and paraglide the Andes mountains or scale Guatape rock on weekends.

Medellín's transformation into a tech hub has attracted digital nomads seeking an affordable yet innovative destination. The cost of living is surprisingly low, allowing you to dine in top-notch restaurants without breaking the bank. Safety has improved significantly, and the healthcare infrastructure is solid. The city's digital nomad community is growing, and the locals are known for their warmth and friendliness.

Lisbon, Portugal - The European Gem

Off to Europe we go, landing in Lisbon, Portugal. Lisbon's historic, old-world charm is complemented by its modern amenities. Coworking spaces in historical buildings like Cowork Central and LACS provide a perfect blend of work and leisure. The cost of living is reasonable, and Portugal's Golden Visa program simplifies the settling process.

The digital nomad community is thriving, with events like Web Summit drawing professionals worldwide. Explore the city's vibrant nightlife, dine on seafood delicacies, and surf along the beautiful coastline. Plus, who could resist those pastéis de nata?

Mexico City, Mexico - The Megalopolis Marvel

Bienvenidos a Mexico City, a bustling megalopolis where ancient history meets modern innovation. While the cost of living varies, it's generally affordable, with street food being a delicious bargain. Mexico City's digital nomad community is growing, with opportunities for networking and collaboration. The cost of living here is a bargain, and the city is filled with mainstream and cozy coworking spots like WeWork and Centraal for your fix of reliable internet. Discover Aztec ruins, explore Frida Kahlo's house, and savor mouthwatering tacos al pastor. Mexico City's vibrant culture and rich heritage are matched by a burgeoning tech scene. With world-class food and an exciting arts scene, this city never stops moving.

Tbilisi, Georgia - The Hidden Gem

Now, let's explore the hidden gem of the Caucasus, Tbilisi, Georgia. It may not be on everyone's radar, but it's quickly becoming a digital nomad hotspot. Affordable co-working spaces like Impact Hub and Terminal provide a productive environment. The cost of living is astonishingly low, and Georgian cuisine is a delightful surprise. It's not the first place that comes to mind for most, but that's what makes it special. You'll be welcomed with open arms by the friendly locals. The city has a bohemian atmosphere, and the growing digital nomad community is welcoming and tight-knit, hosting meet-ups and events often. Explore Tbilisi's unique architecture, ancient churches, and vibrant arts scene while indulging in delectable cuisine will have your taste buds dancing.

Ho Chi Minh City, Vietnam - The Foodie's Paradise

Let's jet over to Ho Chi Minh City, Vietnam. This foodie's paradise boasts a low cost of living and mouth-watering street food on every corner, both delectable and economical. The digital nomad community here is engaging; you'll find plenty of networking events. Coworking spaces like DreamPlex and Toong offer excellent facilities designed for productivity. Explore bustling, vibrant markets, visit historic landmarks to soak in the rich history, and meander through beautiful landscapes on your weekends off. Don't forget to try pho, Vietnam's iconic noodle soup at various local restaurants to discover which is the best.

Budapest, Hungary - The European Bargain

In the heart of Europe, Budapest, Hungary, offers affordability with a touch of grandeur. The cost of living here is remarkably low, and the city boasts stunning architecture. Budapest's digital nomad scene is growing, with coworking spaces like KAPTÁR and Loffice that provide a comfortable work environment and a welcoming community. Soak in the city's famous thermal baths and discover its rich history. Enjoy hearty, gourmet Hungarian dishes between work sessions, events, and meet-ups.

Cape Town, South Africa - The Nature Lover's Dream

Heading south to Cape Town, South Africa, you'll be surrounded by stunning natural beauty. Cape Town's breathtaking landscapes and diverse culture make it a standout destination. The cost of living is moderate, and the city is well-equipped with amenities. It boasts reliable internet and scenic views at coworking spaces like Workshop17 and Inner City Ideas Cartel. Cape Town's community of digital nomads is expanding, drawn by the city's diverse culture and outdoor adventures, from safaris to breathtaking coastal drives and meet-up events to wine tours and outdoor adventures await in Cape Town.

Barcelona, Spain - The Beachside Oasis

Our next stop is Barcelona, Spain - a sun-soaked city that combines work with relaxation by the Mediterranean Sea. The cost of living may be higher, but it's balanced by a high-quality lifestyle that makes it worth it. Barcelona's coworking spaces like OneCoWork and Betahaus provide an inspiring work environment and a mix of work and play. The city's digital nomad community thrives on beach days and tapas nights. With its unique cityscape and vibrant atmosphere, Barcelona has its own magnetic charm. Explore Gaudí's architecture, stroll along La Rambla, and savor tapas by the sea. Barcelona's digital nomad community enjoys beach meet-ups and collaborative events.

Belgrade, Serbia - The Affordable European Gem

Belgrade surprises with its affordability and vibrant nightlife. Co-working spaces like Smart Office and Nova Iskra offer modern amenities and a community feel. The cost of living is remarkably low, and the city's cafe culture is ideal for remote work. Belgrade's digital nomad population is growing, hosting events and gatherings. Discover the city's history, indulge in Serbian cuisine, party in floating clubs, and dance the night away in this Balkan beauty.

Playa del Carmen, Mexico - The Beachside Retreat

Let's dive back into Mexico, but this time, it's all about the beach life in Playa del Carmen to add a coastal vibe to the remote work landscape. The cost of living here is reasonable, and you'll be tempted to work with your toes in the sand. This coastal town offers coworking spaces like Nest and WorkZone with incredible beachfront locations. Playa del Carmen's digital nomad community is on the rise, with beach meet-ups and events. Snorkel in the crystal-clear waters of cenotes, explore ancient Mayan ruins, and unwind with a margarita in beachfront bars- it's all part of the Playa del Carmen experience.

So, there you have it, an epic journey across the globe, from tropical paradises to European gems and hidden treasures. Each destination offers something unique, making it perfect for digital nomads seeking adventure, affordability, and a strong sense of community. Whether you're into beach vibes, cultural exploration, or simply chasing the sun, these destinations have got you covered. Of course, there are countless others for you to explore, so do your research and figure out which destinations fit your vibe!

CHAPTER FOURTEEN

———

LIVING LIKE A LOCAL

Embrace, Connect, and Immerse

L et's unlock the full potential of your adventures as we explore the awe-inspiring world of cultural immersion. Open your heart, broaden your horizons, and truly experience the magic of connecting with different cultures. This chapter will explore the power of embracing local vibes, forging genuine connections, understanding customs, savoring mouthwatering authentic cuisine, and practicing responsible tourism. So, grab your open mind and let's embark on this incredible journey together!

Embrace the Local Vibe: Picture this: you're in a new place, where the air buzzes with energy, a whole different world waiting to be explored. It's time to leave your assumptions and preconceived notions at the door and immerse yourself fully in the local vibes. Feel the pulse of the city, the rhythm of life that flows through its streets. Envelop yourself in the rhythm of the city, the cadence of the countryside, or the tranquility of a remote village. Take in the sights, sounds, and flavors surrounding you. Allow yourself to be fully present and curious. Engage with locals, initiate conversations, and be open to new experiences. Remember, every destination has its own unique flavor, and it's up to you to savor it. Embrace the new rhythm and the different way of life, and let it expand your perspective.

Forge Genuine Connections Through Curiosity: The real magic of cultural immersion is all about connecting profoundly with the people who call that place home. It's about transcending the superficial and diving into the depths of human connection. Approach each encounter with genuine curiosity and an open mind. Step out of your comfort zone and seek opportunities to engage with the locals, start conversations, and open yourself up to the richness of their stories and culture. Attend local events, participate in community projects, or simply start chatting with someone who looks intriguing at a neighborhood café. Embrace the power of a smile, a warm greeting, or a simple gesture of kindness to bridge the gap and create bonds that transcend borders. You'll be amazed at the stories, insights, and friendships blossoming when you open yourself to genuine connections. Be genuinely interested in their experiences, traditions, and customs. Share a smile, ask questions, and listen with an open heart. In these moments of connection, bridges are built, and the beauty of our shared humanity shines through.

Understand and Appreciate Customs: To truly connect with a culture, we must strive to understand, respect, and appreciate their customs. Learn a few key phrases in the local language, familiarize yourself with their traditions, and observe how they navigate daily life. Take the time to learn about their traditions, rituals, history, values, and social norms. Show respect by following their customs, especially if they differ from yours, and seek to understand the reasons behind them. Immerse yourself in their stories, legends, and historical heritage. By doing this, you'll gain a deeper understanding of their culture and foster meaningful connections with the people around you. Step into their shoes, see the world through their eyes and embrace the beauty of their traditions. Engage in meaningful conversations with locals, ask about their customs, and listen to their stories. This deepens your understanding, fosters empathy, and strengthens the bonds you create. By cultivating understanding and respect, we create a space for connection and bridge the gaps between our diverse worlds.

Feast on Authentic Culinary Delights: Food is not just nourishment for the body; it's a gateway to a culture's heart and soul. Leave your comfort zone in the rearview mirror and drive full-speed ahead into the local gastronomy. Let your taste buds travel through time and space by experiencing culinary treasures that are a part of the cultural tapestry of the places you explore. Try street food, visit traditional markets, and savor dishes that have been passed down through generations. Food has a way of bringing people together and offering a taste of the local culture like nothing else. Let the food be a conduit for connection, a way of understanding the history, the passion, and the love that goes into every bite. Venture beyond the tourist traps and seek out local eateries, street vendors, and unique family-run restaurants that are off the beaten path. Let your taste buds dance to the flavors, textures, and aromas that define the local cuisine. As you explore the culinary delights, you'll discover the true essence of the culture and honor the heritage, creativity, and craftsmanship that go into each dish.

Cultivate Responsible Travel Practices: As conscious travelers, it's crucial to be mindful of our impact on the places we visit. We are responsible for positively impacting the world around us as we venture through it. Engage in responsible and ethical tourism practices that respect the environment, culture, and local communities, leaving a footprint of kindness and respect. Seek experiences that promote sustainability by choosing eco-friendly accommodations, and preserve the destination's cultural heritage by seeking experiences that embrace and celebrate that unique heritage. Support local businesses, artisans, and social enterprises to contribute to the community's well-being. Respect the environment by minimizing waste, conserving resources, and treading lightly on the natural wonders of the land. By traveling with intention and care, we become stewards of the places we love. We contribute to the sustainable growth of these beautiful places and the preservation of these precious cultures for future generations to cherish.

So, fellow adventurers, let cultural immersion be the compass that guides you to the most profound experiences of your life—navigating you through the depths of human connection, understanding, and growth. Embrace the local vibes, forge genuine connections, understand customs, indulge in exquisite authentic cuisine, and practice responsible tourism. In doing so, you'll enrich your life and become a catalyst for empathy, unity, appreciation, and global harmony. So, get out there, let the world become your classroom, and immerse yourself in an endless variety of cultural experiences to let your journey be one of discovery, connection, and understanding.

CHAPTER FIFTEEN

———

ACHIEVING AFFORDABLE ADVENTURES

A lright, my adventurous amigos, it's time to crack the code on traveling the world without breaking the bank. In this chapter, we'll dive headfirst into the world of budget travel, where every dollar counts and every experience is worth its weight in gold. Picture this: a world where your travel dreams can be realized without breaking the bank. So, if you're ready to stretch your travel budget like a rubber band and create unforgettable memories on a shoestring, buckle up because we're about to embark on a journey of affordable adventures!

Unlocking Affordable Accommodations

When finding a place to lay your weary head, imagine finding a cozy haven that doesn't drain your travel budget. Well, it's within your reach! There's a treasure trove of options for budget-conscious travelers. The key is to strike a balance and find that sweet spot between comfort and cost, where your wallet and wanderlust can coexist, creating a home away from home without breaking the bank.

Practice Mindfulness in Decision-Making: Take a mindful approach to finding accommodations. Pause, breathe, and consider what truly matters to you during your travels. Reflect on your budget, values, and desired experiences. Mindful decision-making ensures that your choices align with your priorities so you can make the most of affordable accommodations:

Practice Gratitude for the Simple Things: As you search for affordable accommodations, remember to appreciate the beauty in simplicity. Instead of focusing solely on luxurious amenities, seek out places that offer comfort, safety, and an opportunity to connect with others. Gratitude opens your eyes to the abundance of options available.

Explore Alternative Accommodations: Think beyond hotels and consider alternatives like vacation rentals, homestays, or even camping for a unique and budget-friendly experience.

Consider vacation rentals: Look for affordable vacation rentals where you can enjoy more space, privacy, and the comforts of home at a reasonable price.

Explore the Hostel Haven: Look for accommodations that foster a sense of belonging. Hostels, for example, often create a warm and inclusive atmosphere where travelers from different backgrounds can come together and form meaningful connections. Feeling like you belong is priceless. Hostels are not just for backpackers anymore. They offer budget-friendly options with vibrant communal spaces, creating opportunities to meet fellow travelers and share unforgettable experiences.

Seek Authentic Connections Through House Sitting: When choosing accommodations, consider the opportunity for genuine connections with locals and fellow travelers. House-sitting, for instance, allows you to live like a local and build relationships with the community. Imagine living in someone else's cozy home, rent-free, while caring for their furry friends or tending to their plants. House-sitting allows you to immerse yourself in a local community, enjoy a home's comforts, and save on accommodation costs.

Get Cozy in Co-Living Spaces: Experience the perfect blend of affordability and community by exploring the world of co-living spaces. These innovative accommodations provide shared living spaces, communal activities, and a chance to connect with like-minded individuals from around the globe. Join co-living communities where you can share a space with like-minded individuals, fostering connections and creating a supportive network in a cost-effective environment.

Plan Ahead: Booking your accommodations in advance can often lead to better deals and discounts. Research your destination, check out various accommodation options, and secure your spot early to snag the best prices.

Be a Savvy Researcher: Dive deep into the vast ocean of online resources to find the best deals and hidden gems in the world of affordable accommodations. Some travel sites and apps allow you to track your trip to tell you when prices would likely be the lowest, and others offer low price guarantees that reimburse you if the accommodation you book drops in price after you booked it.

Be Flexible with Dates and Locations: Flexibility with your travel dates can lead to significant savings. Plan your trips during non-peak seasons or travel mid-week to take advantage of lower rates and avoid crowds. Also, exploring lesser-known destinations can significantly lower your accommodation expenses. Keep your options open and be willing to venture off the beaten path occasionally.

Utilize Online Booking Platforms: Scour the web for discounts, promotions, and last-minute deals on accommodation booking websites to find great bargains. Take advantage of online platforms specializing in budget accommodations like hostels, guesthouses, and budget hotels. These platforms often offer competitive rates and user reviews to help you make informed decisions. Speaking of reviews, it is wise to let the experiences of fellow travelers guide you. Read reviews and ratings to get a sense of the quality and value of different accommodations and areas of a particular destination. This can definitely save you some headaches while on the go.

A personal favorite booking platform is www.purplecowtravel.com

Consider Long-term Stays: Planning an extended stay? If you plan to settle in one place for an extended period, consider long-term rentals or subletting options. These arrangements can offer substantial savings compared to short-term stays. Negotiate with accommodation providers directly to secure discounted rates for longer durations, or consider renting monthly.

Leverage Travel Memberships and Loyalty Programs: Join travel memberships or loyalty programs offered by accommodation providers. These programs can provide exclusive discounts, perks, and rewards that save you money on future stays. I personally leverage a wholesale travel membership from www.Deilio.com

Connect with Local Communities: Engage with locals through online communities, forums, or social media groups to find hidden gems, local recommendations, and even opportunities for accommodation swaps or Couchsurfing. Seek recommendations from locals or fellow travelers who have visited your desired destination. They often have insider tips on affordable yet authentic accommodations.

Follow Travel-Oriented Social Media and Newsletters: Stay updated on travel deals by following social media accounts, joining travel groups, and subscribing to newsletters of travel websites or accommodation providers. Trade Skills for Accommodation: Consider offering your skills or services in exchange for accommodation. Some establishments or fellow travelers may be open to bartering, allowing you to contribute your expertise while enjoying free or discounted lodging.

Support Local Businesses: Consider staying in locally owned accommodations, guesthouses, or family-run establishments. Supporting local businesses benefits the local economy and provides a more authentic and immersive travel experience. Often, family-run establishments offer cozy, often more affordable accommodations and a taste of authentic culture.

Stay Open to Serendipity: Sometimes, the best experiences come unexpectedly. Stay open to serendipity and be willing to adjust your plans if a unique opportunity arises. Serendipitous encounters can lead to extraordinary adventures and introduce you to remarkable people along the way.

Remember, finding affordable accommodations is not just about saving money—it's a puzzle that requires resourcefulness, creativity, and a willingness to explore beyond the beaten path. It will enable you to immerse yourself in new experiences, connect with like-minded travelers, and make memories that will last a lifetime. With these pro tips in your arsenal, you'll have a range of strategies to find affordable accommodations and stretch your travel budget. So, get out there, embrace the adventure, and find your perfect home away from home without breaking the bank.

Cracking the Transportation Code

Ah, the thrill of traversing the globe while keeping your travel expenses in check. Let's face it: getting from point A to point B can be a significant expense when exploring the world. There are myriad ways to navigate the transportation labyrinth without emptying your pockets. To master the art of affordable transportation, be open to travel hacks that can help you snag the best deals. Remember, the journey is just as important as the destination and should be a memorable part of your travel experience, so why not make it an adventure?

As with accommodation, being flexible with your travel dates can unlock budget-friendly options that may make shifting things around a bit worth the challenge. While it's good to plan ahead and take advantage of early booking discounts, stay flexible and be open to last-minute deals. Sometimes, spontaneity can lead to incredible savings.

Fly on off-peak days. Look for flights on different days or times to find the best deals and avoid peak travel periods. Also, consider alternative airports. Look beyond the major airports and consider smaller regional airports nearby. They might offer lower fares and fewer crowds, giving you more bang for your buck. Embrace the power of flexibility. Being open to adjusting your travel dates, times, and even destinations can unlock hidden savings gems.

Use flight comparison websites: Take advantage of online platforms that compare prices across multiple airlines to find the most affordable options without the hassle of searching individually.

Set fare alerts: Let technology do the work by setting up fare alerts for your desired destinations. Watch for flash sales, error fares, and discounted flights. You'll receive notifications when prices drop, helping you secure the best deals.

Be strategic with layovers: If you're open to a little extra adventure, consider flights with layovers strategically, as they can often be cheaper than direct flights. Sometimes, a longer layover can give you an opportunity for a bonus adventure by exploring a new city in the middle of your journey without the added cost of a separate flight.

Fly with budget airlines: Explore budget airlines offering lower fares, but be mindful of additional fees and restrictions. Pack light and avoid baggage fees. Traveling with just a carry-on can help you avoid expensive baggage fees. Plus, it's liberating to have fewer things weighing you down. Be mindful that some budget airlines charge for carry-on bags to keep their main fares low, so compare flight prices with that in mind.

Explore alternative modes of travel: Trains, buses, or even carpooling services can provide cost-effective alternatives, especially for shorter distances. It's like taking a scenic route while saving some cash.

Sign up for airline newsletters and follow airlines on social media: Airlines often announce special promotions and exclusive deals on their social media channels. Stay connected and be the first to snatch those discounted tickets. Stay informed about exclusive deals and promotions by subscribing to airline newsletters and keeping an eye on their social media announcements.

Maximize travel rewards: Take advantage of travel rewards programs and credit cards that offer miles or points. Rack up those travel rewards points like a boss. Accumulate them strategically to redeem free or discounted flights in the future.

Utilize travel credit cards: Use credit cards that offer travel rewards or cashback on flight purchases to save money in the long run. Especially travel cards that offer the opportunity to transfer points to strategic travel partners to multiply the benefits exponentially.

Rent a vehicle: If you're staying in a destination for an extended period, renting a car or van may be more cost-effective than relying on public transportation.

Embrace the road trip for nearby destinations, share costs with friends or family and enjoy the freedom of the open road.

By incorporating these pro tips into your travel planning, you'll be able to navigate the world of transportation with a keen eye for savings. Remember, every dollar saved on transportation means more money for amazing experiences and adventures at your destination.

Maximizing Experiences While Minimizing Expenses

Who says extraordinary experiences and lasting memories must come with an extraordinary price tag? Let me tell you a little secret, my savvy sojourners: the world is teeming with free and low-cost adventures waiting to be discovered. Seek out free attractions, dive into the rich cultural tapestry of local markets, and immerse yourself in the vibrant energy of street festivals. And let's not forget the gastronomic delights! Indulge in the mouth watering world of street food, where affordability and flavor collide. Let's explore some pro-tips for maximizing experiences while minimizing expenses.

Seek out free attractions like a treasure hunter: Research and explore parks, gardens, historical landmarks, viewpoints, and public spaces that offer breathtaking views and entertainment without an entrance fee. Uncover hidden gems in your destination that won't cost you a dime.

Get lost in local markets: Immerse yourself in the vibrant atmosphere of bustling local markets, where you can find fresh produce, handmade crafts, unique souvenirs, and authentic cultural experiences.

Take advantage of free city and walking tours: Lace up your shoes and join free walking tours guided by passionate, enthusiastic locals who share their knowledge, insights, and fascinating stories about the city's history, culture, and landmarks. It's like having a personal tour guide without opening your wallet. Many cities also offer free audio guides that provide valuable insights and historical context. It's like having your own digital tour guide at your fingertips.

Discover nature's playground: Venture into the great outdoors and discover nature's beauty through hiking trails, parks, and beaches. You can enjoy a refreshing break from the bustling city by hiking, biking, or simply strolling through green spaces. Bask in the natural wonders of community gardens or nature reserves where you can enjoy the beauty of the great outdoors without spending a dime.

Connect with the community through cultural events: Immerse yourself in local traditions and festivals, where you can experience the vibrant energy of the community. By attending free concerts and art exhibitions, you can connect with locals and experience the true spirit of the place without breaking the bank. Tap into the pulse of the city by seeking out free cultural performances. Watch out for street performances or open-air events where you can enjoy live music, dance, or theater without a price tag.

Learn something new: Attend free workshops, language classes, or cultural exchanges to immerse yourself in the local traditions and gain new skills.

Follow your taste buds: Discover the city's flavors by indulging in affordable street food. Sample the culinary wonders of street vendors, allowing each bite to take you on a budget-friendly culinary adventure.

Visit museums and attractions on free days: Many museums and attractions offer free or discounted admission on specific days or during certain hours. Plan your visits accordingly and soak up the art and history, expanding your cultural horizons without emptying your wallet.

Take advantage of city passes: Invest in city passes that offer discounted, free, or bundled admission to multiple attractions. It's like unlocking a treasure trove of experiences at a fraction of the cost.

Embrace the art of haggling: In some cultures, bargaining is a way of life. Channel your inner negotiator and try your hand at haggling for souvenirs or goods at local markets. You might just snag a great deal.

Volunteer or participate in community activities: Give back to the community and make a difference by volunteering or participating in local activities. It's a meaningful way to connect with locals and create lasting memories.

Connect with fellow travelers and locals: Join online travel communities or attend meetups to connect with like-minded adventurers who can share tips and even split costs for certain activities. Strike up conversations with friendly locals, and be open to their suggestions. Ask for recommendations, and let the locals guide you to hidden spots, secret adventures, and off-the-beaten-path experiences that are both enriching and budget-friendly.

Pack a picnic: Save money on meals by grabbing some fresh local produce and goodies from markets. Enjoy a delightful picnic with local treats in a scenic park or by the waterfront, savoring delicious food while enjoying the view. Save more on food expenses by packing snacks and a reusable water bottle, allowing you to stay energized and hydrated on your adventures.

Prioritize experiences over material possessions: Focus on creating meaningful memories and immersing yourself in local culture rather than splurging on material things that won't bring lasting fulfillment. Capture the essence of your experiences through photographs and create lasting memories. Take stunning photos of iconic landmarks and charming streets, preserving your experiences without spending a dime.

Explore local neighborhoods: Venture beyond the tourist hotspots and discover the charm of local neighborhoods. You'll find authentic experiences, local cuisine, and hidden gems off the beaten path that are often overlooked but offer unique experiences.

Tap into the sharing economy: Utilize platforms for couchsurfing or house-swapping to find affordable accommodations and connect with locals who can offer valuable insights and recommendations. Consider house-sitting, home exchanges, or renting rooms from locals to save money on accommodations while immersing yourself in the local lifestyle.

Be open to serendipity: Leave room for spontaneous adventures, unplanned explorations, and unexpected encounters, allowing the magic of the moment to guide you to remarkable experiences.

Utilize technology: Leverage travel apps and websites to discover free guided tours, walking routes, and local recommendations for budget-friendly activities.

Embrace the joy of simple pleasures: Find joy in watching a sunset, strolling through local neighborhoods, or enjoying a leisurely afternoon people-watching in a park or relaxing on a beach – it's often the simplest moments that leave a lasting impact.

Plan visits during off-peak seasons: Save on accommodation, transportation, and attractions by planning your trips during less busy times when prices tend to be lower. Also, "shoulder season," which is right before or right after the peak seasons, can provide discounts and less traffic for the main attractions. While at your destination, time your activities schedule strategically. Enjoy happy hours, discounted lunch menus, or off-peak hours at popular attractions to save money on dining and activities.

Embrace the power of research: Plan your itinerary ahead of time, uncovering free events, discounts, and promotions happening during your visit.

As you venture into the realm of affordable adventures armed with these budget travel strategies, a world of exploration awaits you. From finding the perfect wallet-friendly accommodations to cracking the transportation code and mastering the art of experiences on a budget, you're equipped with the knowledge to explore the world without draining your funds. Remember, it's not about how much money you spend but the experiences you create and the memories you cherish. The best moments in life are often the simplest and most authentic ones. You hold the keys to a world of affordable wanderlust, so go forth, embrace the adventure, make the most of every moment, and let the joy of discovery outweigh the size of your wallet.

CHAPTER SIXTEEN

———

THE ART OF SLOW TRAVEL

Immerse, Discover, and Savor the Journey

In this fast-paced world, everything seems to move at the speed of light. Everything is whizzing by us as we rush through the day, pack every minute with tasks and to-do lists, and hustle from place to place every minute of every day. This can leave any person feeling frazzled, stressed, and longing for a reprieve from the digital noise and tiny glowing screens.

The concept of slow travel offers a refreshing alternative. It's the antidote to the fast-paced, always-on lifestyle that often consumes us. It's a chance to step off the treadmill, take a breath, and embrace a slower pace, providing a powerful avenue for growth and enhancing the lives of those who embrace it.

Slow travel allows us to tune ourselves to the present moment and engage with the world around us in a more conscious and meaningful way. It's not just a physical journey; it's a state of mind, a way of immersing oneself in the beauty of every moment. It's all about taking the time to truly soak in the essence of a place and connect with it on a deeper level, allowing us to break free from the fast-paced, hectic routines of modern life and truly connect with ourselves and the world around us.

Remote workers, in particular, have the unique opportunity to embrace slow travel. By slowing down and taking the time to truly explore our surroundings, we open ourselves up to a world of discovery. With the flexibility to work from anywhere, they can tap into the essence of a destination and fully experience its offerings. Remote workers can broaden their perspectives and nurture their creativity by slowing down and savoring the journey. It allows them to step outside their comfort zones, embrace new cultures, and create meaningful connections. By immersing themselves in the local lifestyle, remote workers can gain fresh perspectives and unlock a wellspring of inspiration for their work.

Slow travel is more than just ticking attractions off a list like a mindless tourist; it's a mindset that encourages you to dive deep into the local culture, connect with the people, and discover the hidden gems that make a place special. It is a profound invitation to immerse oneself in the journey and savor the experience with a deep sense of inner connection. Release the need to rush from one place to another; instead, choose to savor each experience and allow it to unfold in its natural rhythm. These are the moments that bring richness and meaning to our travels. They allow us to truly experience a destination beyond the superficial snapshots a hurried tourist captures.

Picture this: you find yourself strolling through the cobblestone streets of a charming little town, far away from the tourist traps. The air is thick with the aroma of fresh produce and street vendors peddling their wares. You are chatting with the locals at the bustling market or sipping a cup of coffee in a quaint café while watching the world go by. You engage with the friendly vendors, learning about their traditions and listening to the stories embedded in their craft. And when hunger strikes, you head to the street food stalls, where the sizzle of grills and the vibrant colors of the dishes beckon you closer. As you slow down and savor the journey, you'll find moments of clarity and insights that can only arise when we give ourselves the space to listen, observe, and be present.

Now, I'm not saying you must travel at a snail's pace or stay in one place indefinitely. Slow travel is a mindset, a way of approaching your adventures with intention and mindfulness. It's about finding a balance between exploration and immersion, between the excitement of new horizons and the joy of being rooted in a community, even if just for a short while.

As we slow down, we become attuned to the rhythms of the community. We notice the subtle details that would have otherwise escaped us—the way the sunlight dances through ancient alleyways, the laughter of children playing in a neighborhood square, and the heartfelt conversations shared over a cup of tea with a newfound friend.

This form of travel invites us to savor the journey not just externally but internally as well. It becomes an opportunity for self-reflection, personal growth, and deepening our consciousness. As we detach from the incessant distractions of the digital world, we create space for inner exploration, quiet contemplation, and a reconnection with our true selves.

In the process of slow travel, we may encounter discomfort and challenges. We may face language barriers, cultural differences, or moments of solitude. These moments of discomfort, however, offer us the chance to cultivate resilience and grow as individuals. It means surrendering to the flow of the journey and allowing ourselves to be fully present, even when faced with unfamiliar situations or challenging experiences. We discover our inner strength and resourcefulness by leaning into vulnerability and embracing the unknown.

In the practice of slow travel, we become aware of the interconnectedness of all things. We recognize that we are not separate observers but integral parts of the tapestry of life. We witness the threads that connect us to the local communities—the shared joys, struggles, and aspirations that unite us as human beings.

Slow travel is about embracing the authentic, the unexplored, and the unique aspects of a destination. To truly immerse ourselves, we must be willing to step out of our comfort zones and fully engage with the local community. This might mean participating in cultural activities, attending local festivals, or volunteering for local causes. It may also mean joining a traditional dance, witnessing a religious ceremony, or learning a craft from local artisans. By doing so, we gain a firsthand understanding of the place and its people. These immersive encounters create lasting memories and leave us with a deeper understanding and appreciation for the diversity and beauty of our world.

By embracing a slower pace, we allow ourselves to be present in the moment, to truly listen, and to engage with the world around us. We let go of the pressure to constantly achieve, accomplish, and fill our schedule with back-to-back activities. We release the need to be productive at all times and instead prioritize rest, relaxation, and self-care. Slow travel becomes an opportunity to recharge our batteries, to reconnect with ourselves, and to nourish our souls. We cultivate an attitude of curiosity, openness, and acceptance, knowing that the most profound experiences often arise when we least expect them.

So, my fellow travelers, I invite you to embrace the art of slow travel. Let go of the need to cover vast distances in hastened timelines and immerse yourself in the present moment. Be fully present, fully alive, and fully receptive to the wonders that unfold before you. In doing so, you will not only discover the world but also yourself—unveiling the depths of your being and expanding your capacity for love, compassion, empathy, and joy. Let the pace of your travels be guided by curiosity and authenticity, and you'll find that the most memorable moments are often found off the beaten path. May your journey be one of profound awakening and transformation.

CHAPTER SEVENTEEN

MAKING CONNECTIONS

Building a Global Network of Like-Minded Individuals

I magine having a network of friends, colleagues, and fellow adventurers spread across the globe. As remote workers and travelers, our journey becomes even more enriching when we connect with others who share our passion for exploration, growth, and new experiences. We will explore the importance of networking, the power of social media, and how to foster meaningful relationships with people who share your remote work and travel lifestyle. These connections can open doors to exciting opportunities, offer support and guidance, and create a sense of belonging no matter where you are. Let's analyze the ins and outs of creating, building, and nurturing such a network using modern tools and timeless principles of human connection. Trust me, this is the key to unlocking a world of opportunities and epic adventures.

Networking is not just a buzzword; it's the gateway to opportunity and a vital aspect of personal and professional growth. By connecting with other remote workers and travelers, we expand our horizons, gain new perspectives, and tap into a wealth of knowledge and experiences. It's not just about exchanging business cards or collecting contacts on your LinkedIn—it's about connecting with people who share your passions, dreams, and ambitions, establishing and nurturing relationships with individuals who can contribute to your growth and vice versa.

A robust network can open doors you never even knew existed. These connections can lead to collaborative projects, career opportunities, and lifelong friendships. It connects you to resources, insights, and experiences that can propel you forward. Expanding your network allows you to tap into a collective wisdom that enhances your knowledge and expertise. So, recognize the power of networking and embrace it as a fundamental pillar of your personal and professional development.

The key is to approach networking with a genuine desire to connect, collaborate, and contribute. When you focus on building meaningful connections beyond purely superficial levels, the world becomes your playground, filled with endless possibilities. It's about forming authentic relationships with people who can elevate your journey and vice versa.

When connecting with fellow remote workers and travelers, you're tapping into a network of knowledge, experiences, and resources that will enhance your journey. We thrive when surrounded by people who understand us, support us, and inspire us to be our best selves. These connections become your allies, cheerleaders, mentors, and friends, guiding you toward new horizons and helping you overcome challenges along the way.

In today's digital age, social media platforms, online forums, and co-working spaces have become powerful tools for building connections. They provide platforms for remote workers and travelers to meet, share stories, exchange advice, and organize meetups.

We live in a world interwoven with social media, and it's a game-changer. Platforms like Instagram, Facebook, and Twitter have become more than just places to share selfies and cat videos.

They're powerful tools that offer unprecedented opportunities to meet like-minded individuals across borders and time zones, discover new opportunities, and build your global network.

Professional networking sites like LinkedIn can also serve as virtual hubs for building virtual connections with professionals near and far. Leverage the power of technology to bridge distances and create a global network that knows no boundaries. Engage in conversations, share your journey, and seek out individuals who resonate with your aspirations. By actively engaging with these online communities, we can establish and nurture valuable connections in communities of remote workers and travelers who are ready and willing to connect and share their insights. Equally, they provide you with a global platform to establish yourself as a thought leader.

While online platforms are invaluable, there's no substitute for face-to-face interactions. When you're on the move, seek co-working spaces to create meaningful connections in person. Co-working spaces are like magnets for creative minds and nomadic souls. These vibrant hubs bring together remote workers, digital entrepreneurs, and travelers from all walks of life. You'll find a melting pot of ideas, collaborations, and support here. Strike up conversations, attend events and workshops, and immerse yourself in the vibrant energy of these spaces. From shared desks to cozy lounges, co-working spaces provide the perfect backdrop for building relationships and finding potential collaborators who share your drive and enthusiasm.

Attend conferences, seminars, and networking events in your field of interest. Surround yourself with individuals who share your passion and drive. Engage in conversations fully, listen actively, and be genuinely curious about others. Immersing yourself in physical gatherings and communities creates opportunities to establish deeper connections and build lasting relationships. Remember, true connections are forged through personal interactions and shared experiences.

The foundation of any fruitful connection lies in building

genuine and meaningful relationships. Seek to understand others, listen attentively to their stories, and demonstrate empathy and compassion. By showing a sincere interest in their experiences and aspirations, you lay the groundwork for lasting connections. When it comes down to it, it's not about the number of connections you have but the quality. To build a strong network, focus on being a value provider rather than a value extractor. Seek opportunities to assist others, share your expertise, and provide solutions to their challenges.

Building meaningful relationships means being present and investing in the connection. Actively listen, really listen to what they have to say. Pay attention to their needs and offer support without expecting immediate reciprocation. By consistently adding value to others' lives, you build trust and establish yourself as a reliable resource within your network. When you do this, you'll attract people who will inspire, uplift, and support you on your journey. Remember, it's not just about what others can do for you; it's about how you can contribute to their journey, and the more you give, the more you receive in return.

A supportive community is invaluable to your remote work and travel adventure. Surround yourself with individuals who believe in your dreams, challenge you to grow, and offer unwavering support. Foster a supportive community where everyone feels valued, respected, and heard. Be there for one another and offer a helping hand.

Together, you'll create a network that becomes your safety net, sounding board, and biggest source of encouragement. Within this tribe, you will find motivation, inspiration, and a devoted environment to share your triumphs and setbacks. Nurture this community by actively participating, offering assistance, and celebrating the successes of others. By creating a supportive network, we build a community that understands the unique joys and struggles of the remote lifestyle. Together, you can conquer any obstacle that comes your way.

Now, here's where things get really exciting. Building

connections isn't just about having friends to share a beer with. One of the most beautiful aspects of building a global network is the potential for collaboration and shared experiences. It's about finding opportunities to collaborate and create something amazing together. Imagine teaming up with fellow nomads on a project, planning epic group adventures, or even starting a business together. These shared experiences create bonds and memories that will last a lifetime. The possibilities are endless when you join forces with like-minded individuals who share your passion and vision.

A vibrant network comprises individuals with diverse backgrounds, skills, and perspectives. Embrace this diversity and recognize the immense value it brings to your network. Engage in collaborations and projects that leverage the collective strengths of your network. By working together, you can achieve outcomes that surpass what any individual could accomplish alone. Embrace the power of collaboration and harness the collective genius of your network to unlock new levels of success.

Building a network is not a one-time endeavor; it's an ongoing process. Continually seek opportunities to expand your network, learn from others, and contribute to their growth. Stay curious and open-minded, always seeking new knowledge and insights.

As you embark on building a global network of like-minded individuals, remember the words of wisdom: "You become the average of the five people you spend the most time with." By networking, engaging in meaningful relationships, and fostering a supportive community, you elevate your potential and that of those around you.

Surround yourself with people who inspire you, collaborate on exciting projects, and together, create unforgettable experiences. So, get out there and connect with the tribe that will take your remote work and travel lifestyle to the next level.

Congratulations, fellow adventurer! You've now unlocked the tools, the mindset, and the know-how to build a global network of like-minded individuals. By embracing the power of social media, actively participating in online communities, and fostering meaningful relationships that inspire and support you, you're tapping into a world of endless opportunities for collaboration and shared experiences. Surround yourself with a community that uplifts you and encourages your growth. And don't forget the magic of adding more value than you extract. By embracing these principles, you'll create a network that propels you forward, amplifies your impact, and makes your remote work and travel journey an unforgettable adventure. So, get out there, connect with like-minded individuals, and let your network become a force that transforms your dreams into reality.

CHAPTER EIGHTEEN

HEALTH AND WELLNESS ON THE ROAD

Maintaining a Balanced Lifestyle

Welcome to the exciting world of maintaining health and wellness while traveling and working remotely. In this chapter, we'll explore practical strategies and tips to help you prioritize your physical and mental well-being while on the road. We'll cover everything from staying active and incorporating exercise into your routine to managing stress and seeking healthcare resources. We will equip you with the knowledge and tools to thrive in your nomadic journey. Get ready to discover how to cultivate and maintain a balanced, vibrant, and fulfilling lifestyle as you embark on your nomadic journey.

Staying Active and Embracing Movement: Maintaining an active lifestyle is crucial not only for your physical well-being but also for your mental and emotional vitality. It is essential for your overall well-being as a human, regardless of where you are. Find ways to embrace movement and incorporate physical activity into your daily routine, whether it's exploring a new city on foot, engaging in local recreational activities, or practicing yoga in your hotel room; seize every opportunity to keep your body in motion. Embrace the adventure of your surroundings and engage in activities that keep you moving. Remember, even small bursts of physical activity throughout the day can significantly affect your energy levels and overall fitness. By making physical activity a priority, you not only boost your overall health but also enhance your productivity and zest for life.

The Power of a Healthy Lifestyle: Maintaining a healthy lifestyle is crucial to your overall well-being and success as a remote worker and traveler. While nourishing your body with wholesome food and engaging in regular physical activity are two main pillars of a healthy lifestyle, it also encompasses various other aspects, including mental well-being and emotional resilience. By embracing healthy habits and making conscious choices, you can optimize your performance, enhance your productivity, and cultivate a positive mindset. Remember, a healthy lifestyle forms the foundation for your journey toward personal and professional fulfillment.

Cultivating Wholehearted Living: Wholehearted living is about embracing imperfections, cultivating self-compassion, and living authentically. It is an invitation to show up fully, without pretenses or masks, and to embrace all aspects of ourselves. As a remote worker and traveler, wholehearted living means honoring your unique journey, being true to your values, and engaging in practices that nurture your mind, body, and spirit. It's about embracing self-care, setting boundaries, and prioritizing your well-being.

The nomadic lifestyle can bring its fair share of challenges and uncertainties, so you may encounter various stressors along your journey. It's essential to prioritize self-care and develop effective strategies for managing stress and cultivating resilience. Find activities that help you relax and recharge, such as journaling, practicing gratitude, self-reflection, or taking a soothing bath. Set boundaries and create dedicated time for self-care in your schedule. Embrace mindfulness practices, such as meditation and deep breathing, to anchor yourself in the present moment and alleviate anxiety. Prioritize self-care rituals that replenish your energy and restore your inner balance. Practice positive affirmations and visualization techniques to reframe challenges as opportunities for growth. By managing stress, you unlock the power to navigate challenges with grace and maintain a state of mental well-being, empowering yourself to face any obstacle that comes your way. Remember, taking care of yourself is not selfish— it's a necessary act of self-love that enables you to show up as your best self in all areas of your life for yourself and others.

Navigating Healthcare and Medical Resources: When it comes to healthcare on the road, being proactive and well-prepared is vital. While traveling, it's important to be knowledgeable and resourceful and have access to healthcare resources wherever your adventures lead you. Research and identify public health infrastructure in your destinations ahead of time. Familiarize yourself with local clinics, hospitals, and medical professionals. Understand the necessary vaccinations and precautions for each location you plan to visit. Carry essential medications and maintain a comprehensive medical kit to address minor health concerns. Additionally, consider obtaining comprehensive travel insurance to safeguard your well-being. By prioritizing your health and accessing necessary healthcare resources, you can enjoy peace of mind and focus on making the most of your nomadic lifestyle.

Nutrition and Eating Well: Maintaining a balanced and nourishing diet while traveling can present its own set of challenges. However, with conscious choices and mindful planning, you can fuel your body with wholesome food and optimize your overall health and well-being. While exploring new cultures and cuisines is part of the adventure, be mindful of your food choices. Prioritize nutrition by incorporating nutrient-rich foods such as fruits, vegetables, lean proteins, and whole grains into your meals. Explore farm-to-table restaurants for exquisite yet nutritious meals. Seek out local markets and grocery stores where you can find fresh and nutrient-dense options such as fresh, local produce to infuse your diet with vibrant flavors and essential nutrients. Stay hydrated by carrying a reusable water bottle and prioritizing daily water intake. Remember, nourishing your body with wholesome foods will fuel your energy and keep you feeling vibrant.

Honoring Mind-Body Connection: Your physical and mental well-being are intricately connected; nurturing both is essential for a balanced life. Engage in activities that promote mindfulness, such as yoga or meditation, to cultivate awareness of your body and mind. Listen to your body's cues, prioritize rest and sleep, and nourish yourself with wholesome food. Remember, honoring the mind-body connection creates a strong foundation for overall well-being.

Navigating Emotional Resilience: The nomadic lifestyle can bring its share of challenges and emotional ups and downs. Cultivating emotional resilience is crucial in navigating these experiences with grace and strength. Practice self-compassion and self-acceptance, allowing yourself to feel and process emotions without judgment. Seek support from trusted friends, mentors, or therapists when needed. Remember, resilience is not about suppressing emotions but acknowledging them and choosing how to respond.

Building a Supportive Community: Navigating health and wellness while traveling can be easier when you have a supportive community. Connect with like-minded individuals who share your commitment to a balanced lifestyle. Join online forums, attend local meetups or yoga classes in a local park, and engage with fellow travelers and remote workers. Share your experiences, challenges, and tips with one another. A supportive community can provide encouragement, accountability, and valuable insights to help you on your health and wellness journey.

Rest and Recovery for Optimal Performance: Amid your exciting adventures, don't overlook the importance of rest and recovery. Traveling can be physically and mentally demanding, and adequate sleep is the foundation of your well-being and performance, so prioritize quality sleep. Create a restful environment with optimal sleep conditions in your accommodations; establish a bedtime routine and practice good sleep hygiene. Allow yourself moments of relaxation and downtime to recharge your batteries. Carve out time for restorative practices such as taking breaks, enjoying nature, or engaging in hobbies that bring you joy and rejuvenation. A well-rested body and mind are essential for peak performance and overall well-being. By honoring rest and recovery, you enhance your physical and mental health and unlock your full potential as a nomadic explorer.

Maintaining health and wellness on the road is a continuous journey that requires mindful choices and intentional actions. Prioritize your physical and mental well-being by incorporating exercise, practicing self-care, seeking healthcare resources, and nourishing your body with nutritious foods. Embrace rest and recovery as essential components of a balanced lifestyle. And remember, building a supportive community can provide guidance and encouragement along the way. Take charge of your health and well-being, and let it enhance your nomadic journey to its fullest potential.

CHAPTER NINETEEN

———

EMBRACING ADVENTURE

Thrilling Experiences in the Great Outdoors

Within each of us lies a deep longing for exploration and discovery. Embrace your inner explorer and venture into the great outdoors. Adventure awaits in every corner of the globe, from lush rainforests to snow-capped mountains and everything in between. From navigating rugged terrains to diving into crystal-clear waters, there are endless opportunities to challenge yourself and expand your comfort zone. By stepping outside the familiar, you'll uncover hidden strengths, build resilience, and cultivate a growth mindset that propels you toward success. Whether hiking through breathtaking landscapes, conquering challenging trails, or engaging in water sports like surfing or kayaking, there's an adventure for everyone. Embrace the unknown and let the thrill of exploration drive you forward.

Imagine stepping out of your comfort zone and into a world of exhilarating adventures. We're about to dive into the heart-pounding, pulse-racing, and utterly electrifying activities available in different corners of the globe. We're talking about those uncharted territories where human courage dances with endurance. From soaring through the sky to delving deep into the ocean's mysteries, the thrill-seeker in you is in for a treat. This is where we embrace the true thrill of adventure. Whether you're a newbie taking your first steps or a seasoned pro looking for the next adrenaline fix, we're about to dive into the world of outdoor excitement. Get ready to learn about the secrets of safely planning and participating in these activities, exploring natural wonders, water sports, and so much more. But remember, these exciting adventures come with a responsibility – to travel safely and sustainably with a conscious mind to respect the environment. Let's dive in!

The world is a treasure trove of natural wonders waiting to be discovered. From magnificent waterfalls to awe-inspiring canyons, nature offers a playground of exploration. Seek out famous landmarks and hidden gems, immerse yourself in the beauty of national parks, and marvel at the wonders of the natural world. Each destination has its unique charm and adventure, so embrace the opportunity to connect with nature on a deeper level.

Nature is the ultimate playground for adventurers. Whether you're an adrenaline junkie or just someone seeking a dash of excitement, there's a world of possibilities out there. Picture yourself zip-lining through lush rainforests in Costa Rica, surrounded by the symphony of nature, where wild orchids scent the air and howler monkeys serenade you from the treetops. Or maybe you'd prefer canyoning in Utah's Zion National Park, a wonderland of red sandstone, where you can choose between gentle strolls or challenging canyon explorations. These locations offer diverse experiences, each providing a chance to witness Mother Earth's grandeur up close.

Nature is also a profound teacher, offering endless inspiration and invaluable lessons. By immersing ourselves in the natural world, we understand our place in the universe more deeply. Observe the intricate ecosystems, witness the harmonious interplay of life, and learn from nature's wisdom. The resilience of a tree enduring storms, the persistence of a river carving its path— lessons that can be applied to our personal and professional journeys. When you immerse yourself in the great outdoors, you tap into the energy and wisdom that permeates every corner of the natural world. From majestic mountains to babbling brooks, from serene forests to expansive oceans, nature reminds us of our interconnectedness and the vast potential within us. Allow the beauty and harmony of nature to inspire and guide you on your adventure-filled journey.

If you seek an adrenaline rush and find your happy place in edge-of-your-seat activities, there's an array of heart-pounding activities to choose from. Whether bungee jumping, paragliding, rock climbing, or skydiving, these experiences will push your limits and make your heart race with excitement. Engage in these activities under the guidance of trained professionals, and remember to trust your abilities. Embrace the thrill, conquer your fears, and create stories that will be told for years to come.

When we engage in activities that demand our full attention and participation, we enter a realm where time fades away, and our awareness merges with the present moment. Adventure becomes a mirror, reflecting our strengths, vulnerabilities, and untapped potential. In these uncharted territories, we tap into our deepest reservoirs of courage, resilience, and resourcefulness, propelling us toward personal growth, self-discovery, and a life lived on our terms. So, dare to dream big, take calculated risks, and be willing to explore uncharted territories.

Have you ever dreamed of soaring with the birds? Paragliding, hang gliding, and skydiving are not just for daredevils. You can conquer the skies in stunning destinations like Interlaken, Switzerland, and Medellin, Colombia. Imagine feeling the crisp mountain air rushing past you with wonder engulfing your vision in every direction. In the Swiss Alps, you can paraglide, hang glide, or even skydive amidst those breathtaking peaks. This is where Felix Baumgartner made history by skydiving from the stratosphere. It's a dream come true for adventure enthusiasts. Paragliding in the mountains surrounding Medellin, you get to take in the beauty of nature with the backdrop of the city in the valley below. The world is your playground in the sky!

If diving into the deep blue ocean intrigues you, explore the Great Barrier Reef in Australia or the Great Blue Hole off the coast of Belize. Snorkeling or scuba diving in either of these aquatic wonders is like entering another world. The vibrant maze of coral formations and diverse marine life are awe-inspiring. You'll swim alongside sea turtles and colorful fish and maybe even spot a reef shark. A little tip: Bring a waterproof camera to capture these incredible moments. But remember, respecting the underwater environment is crucial; we'll talk more about that soon.

Maybe you crave the rush of water without entering the depths. Whitewater rafting, kayaking, and riverboarding are fantastic ways to quench your thirst for adventure. The Futaleufú River in Chile, with its emerald waters and class V rapids, is a mecca for the ultimate thrill-seeking white-water rafting fans. But don't forget the wise words—join certified rafting courses and trust the experienced river guides for a safe journey.

If you want to take on some whitewater thrills and are just getting your feet wet, venture over to Idaho Springs, Colorado, in the USA. Nestled in the Rocky Mountains, a short westerly drive from Denver, Idaho Springs is an outdoor enthusiast's paradise. What sets it apart is the accessibility to some fantastic white water courses that cater to beginners. The Colorado River and Clear Creek meandering through this area offer various levels of white water excitement. It's not just about the adventure; it's also about making memories and connecting with nature. Braving wild rivers has its unique charm, so when you're dancing with the white waters, brace yourself for an unforgettable river journey that's bound to leave you with stories to tell for years to come.

No adventure is complete without a rendezvous with wildlife. Imagine going on a safari in Kenya's Maasai Mara during the Great Migration—thousands of wildebeests and zebras on their timeless journey. Here's a pro tip: Get a local guide who knows the secrets of the savanna. The savannah is teeming with majestic creatures, from lions to elephants. The sight of a lioness and her cubs or a giraffe majestically strolling by is enough to quicken anyone's pulse.

On the other side of the world and home to diverse marine life, unique bird species and iconic giant tortoises, the Galápagos Islands offer an unparalleled opportunity for close encounters with wildlife. If the thought of interacting with pink river dolphins and giant river otters is more intriguing, perhaps you should consider exploring the world's largest rainforest through guided tours and river cruises in the Amazon for an immersive wildlife experience. No matter where you encounter animals in their natural habitats, remember that wildlife observation should always be respectful and ethical.

Windsurfing and kitesurfing take you to the oceans, where the wind is your engine. There's nothing like the sensation of gliding over the water's surface. Venture to the Greek island of Rhodes, where the Meltemi winds set the stage for aquatic magic. If the Caribbean is calling, then perhaps Cabarete in the Dominican Republic or Isla Verde in Puerto Rico are the places to begin your thrilling ballet in windsurfing and kitesurfing. Learning from the pros is the key to mastering these water dances. It's a true adventure where the elements are your allies.

While adventure is fueled by thrills, it comes with risks, so safety is non-negotiable. When planning these adrenaline-pumping activities, always prioritize safety and prepare for potential risks. Research your chosen activity or excursion thoroughly. The trio of proper training, quality gear, and experienced mentors and instructors complete the adventure. Understand the environment and the potential risks involved. It's the difference between a safe thrill and a reckless adventure. Take necessary precautions, such as wearing appropriate gear, carrying first aid kits, and informing others about your plans. Remember, safety is paramount, and proper preparation enhances the enjoyment of your adventure.

As adventurers, we're custodians of nature and are responsible for protecting the environments we explore. Embrace sustainable travel practices to minimize your impact on fragile ecosystems. Leave no trace, respect wildlife habitats, and support local communities through responsible tourism. Like visiting a friend's house, we aim to leave nature as beautiful as we found it. Why does it matter? Picture a pristine forest hike spoiled by litter—it's like a deflated balloon at a party. Every positive action, however small, contributes to the bigger sustainable picture. We're all in this together; each choice we make, like using a reusable water bottle or respecting trail rules, is a step toward a healthier planet and more unforgettable adventures. It's our chance to be Earth's superheroes, one eco-friendly adventure at a time. By taking care of the places we visit, we ensure that future generations can also enjoy the wonders of our planet.

Adventure is not just about the thrill and rush of the moment; it's about creating lasting memories that enrich our lives. Each adventure becomes a chapter in the story of our lives, etching indelible imprints on our hearts and minds. Whether it's conquering a challenging hiking trail, diving into the ocean's depths, or embarking on a soul-stirring journey, each adventure becomes a story worth telling.

As you embark on your adventurous pursuits, savor every experience, capture the moments, and reflect on the lessons learned. The memories we create during our adventures become a tapestry of experiences that define us and shape our outlook on life. Treasure these memories, for they are the building blocks of your extraordinary life. Adventure becomes a vehicle for building a life filled with vibrant experiences and cherished moments.

The world is a treasure trove of thrilling experiences waiting for you. Now, you're the hero of your own story, ready to conquer mountains and rapids, explore the depths, and chase the winds. But always remember, adventure isn't just about personal excitement; it's also our duty to protect the beauty of our planet. So, whether you're a beginner or a pro, go out there and create legendary and unforgettable experiences. The universe is your canvas, and your masterpiece is waiting to be painted!

CHAPTER TWENTY

———

JOURNEY WITHIN

Traveling the Path of Personal Development and Achievement

A s we embark on a transformative exploration of personal growth, let us pause to reflect on the profound impact of travel on our journey of self-discovery. Adventure is not just about seeking thrills; it is a powerful catalyst for personal growth, self-discovery, and transformation. As we traverse the globe, working remotely and immersing ourselves in diverse cultures and experiences, we discover not only the outer beauty of the world but also the inner depths of our being. We unlock the power within us to grow, evolve, and transform. Get ready to unleash the extraordinary potential within you when you let the world become your greatest teacher on this exhilarating voyage.

Let's explore the transformative power of travel, uncovering how it opens doors to new perspectives, cultural diversity, and global awareness. Through self-reflection exercises, we'll witness the extraordinary potential within each of us when we embark on this wondrous journey of self-discovery.

Our exploits are not confined to grand expeditions, extraordinary experiences, or extreme sports; the adventure lifestyle is a mindset that can be integrated into our daily lives. Becoming a gateway to experiencing life fully and breaking free from the limitations of our conditioned existence, an invitation to explore the depths of our being and uncover the vastness of who we truly are.

Your internal adventure begins with cultivating a mindset fueled by curiosity, fearlessness, a hunger for new experiences, an attitude of approaching each moment with openness, and a willingness to explore. Let's delve into how travel can expand our horizons, foster personal development, and ignite the fire of transformation within.

Through travel, we find ourselves presented with fertile ground for self-reflection, affording us endless opportunities to explore our passions, conquer our fears, and tap into our hidden talents. Amidst the awe-inspiring landscapes and bustling city streets, we find moments of stillness to introspect and connect with our innermost selves.

As we navigate unfamiliar landscapes, we develop resilience, adaptability, and a heightened sense of self-reliance. By setting aside dedicated time for self-reflection exercises, such as journaling, meditation, or engaging in creative pursuits, we gain clarity, discover our passions, and uncover the growth areas within us. Embrace these moments of quiet contemplation as they allow you to reassess your values, clarify your goals, and align your actions with your deepest desires. Travel offers a canvas for self-reflection and deep introspection, enabling us to shed limiting beliefs, discover our true purpose, and create a life aligned with our authentic selves.

The spirit of adventure teaches us the invaluable lessons of resilience and adaptability. It presents us with unpredictable challenges and forces us to think on our feet, adapt to new circumstances, and find creative solutions. As you push your boundaries, you'll encounter physical and mental challenges.

Embrace these obstacles as opportunities for growth and development.

Through trials, we develop mental fortitude, tenacity, and the ability to thrive in the face of adversity. By navigating through these obstacles, we develop a resilient mindset that empowers us to overcome hardship in all areas of life. Adventure becomes a training ground for personal growth and a catalyst for developing the mental and emotional fortitude necessary to thrive as we navigate the ever-changing currents of life in a constantly evolving world. This teaches us that vulnerability is not a weakness but a gateway to strength, courage, and growth. Remember, the greatest triumphs often arise from the most challenging experiences.

Embracing adventure takes us beyond the boundaries of our everyday lives and expands our horizons in ways we never thought possible. It is a realm where fear and growth collide. It's natural to feel apprehensive when faced with the unknown, but it is through confronting our fears that we discover our true strength. It's about seeking new experiences, exploring diverse cultures, and immersing ourselves in unfamiliar environments. Embrace fear as a catalyst for growth, a signpost indicating the path to personal evolution.

By facing our fears, we gain the confidence to take on new challenges and create a truly extraordinary life. As you conquer fear, you unlock new levels of courage and resilience that translate into all areas of your life, empowering you to overcome obstacles and achieve greatness.

Growth happens outside of our comfort zones. The adventure lifestyle beckons us to step beyond the boundaries of familiarity and embrace the unknown. By challenging yourself with new activities and experiences, you expand your comfort zone and develop the confidence to tackle greater challenges in all areas of life, bringing you one step closer to reaching your full potential.

The shift to a traveling lifestyle acts as a motivator for transcending the limiting beliefs that hold us back in life. When we engage in thrilling activities and conquer the challenges they present, we defy the boundaries of what we once believed possible. As we push beyond our perceived limits, we shatter the illusions of our conditioning, revealing a reservoir of untapped potential within. The adventure lifestyle teaches us that our true nature is limitless and that we have the power to rewrite the narratives that confine us.

Adventure demands action. It's not enough to dream; you must take bold and decisive action to bring those dreams to life. It teaches us that hesitation and indecision only hinder progress. To seize the opportunities that lie beyond your comfort zone, you must be willing to take leaps of faith, make bold decisions, and embrace the unknown with unwavering determination. Embrace the power of decisive action, and watch as your dreams transform into reality.

Reclaiming control over your life and living it on your terms is the foundation of an adventurous lifestyle. It's about breaking free from societal norms, embracing individuality, and forging your path. Through this spirit, you assert your independence and refuse to settle for a life of mediocrity. Your life of action becomes a declaration of your freedom, an affirmation that you are the architect of your own destiny.

An adventurous lifestyle is synonymous with personal freedom. It liberates you from the constraints of routine, societal expectations, and self-imposed limitations. You reclaim your autonomy through your voyage and embrace a life of authenticity and self-expression. Each step on your journey becomes a declaration of your individuality and a testament to your unwavering commitment to living life on your own terms.

One of the greatest gifts of travel is the exposure to diverse cultures that shape our planet. Each destination carries its unique tapestry of traditions, beliefs, and values, offering us an invaluable opportunity to immerse ourselves in the richness of human expression. By engaging with local communities, delighting in their cuisine, and participating in their customs, we cultivate a deep appreciation for the incredible landscape of cultural diversity in our world. We connect with the hearts and souls of people from different backgrounds, forging bonds that transcend language barriers and geographical boundaries. Through these connections, we cultivate empathy, compassion, and a profound understanding of the interconnectedness of all people.

Cultural intelligence is a key element of personal growth during travel. As you venture into different regions and engage with diverse communities, you have the opportunity to cultivate a deep appreciation for cultural nuances and build bridges of understanding. This cultural exchange enriches our lives and allows us to see the world through a new lens. In turn, we develop a heightened global awareness and an understanding that connects us to the collective story of humanity. By embracing cultural immersion, we develop the ability to connect authentically with people from all walks of life. This cultural intelligence enriches your experiences and enhances your interpersonal skills.

Traveling offers the remarkable opportunity to step outside the confines of our familiar surroundings and embrace new points of view. We transcend the limitations of our own perspectives through immersive experiences and encounters with different people and environments. The world becomes our classroom, offering profound lessons and insights that challenge our assumptions, expand our worldview, and deepen our understanding. The experiences we gain while traversing unfamiliar territories challenge our preconceived notions and broaden our horizons. We learn to see the world through a multifaceted lens, gaining insight into the interconnectedness of humanity. This newfound perspective allows us to approach life with greater empathy, compassion, and unity with our fellow human beings.

Living a lifestyle of sustained travel provides an unparalleled opportunity for continuous learning. As we explore new destinations and encounter unfamiliar situations, we are presented with a wealth of knowledge and insights waiting to be discovered. Whether it's learning a new language, understanding local history, or engaging in authentic cultural experiences, every interaction becomes an opportunity for growth and education. By approaching our travels with curiosity and a thirst for knowledge, we expand our intellectual horizons, develop new skills, and become lifelong learners. Travel becomes a transformative educational journey, shaping our perspectives, broadening our understanding, and fostering personal and intellectual growth.

Travel has the power to cultivate gratitude and provide a fresh perspective on life. As we immerse ourselves in different environments and witness the beauty and challenges of the world, we develop a profound sense of appreciation for the blessings in our lives. The experiences we encounter during our travels serve as powerful reminders of the mutuality of humanity and the incredible diversity that exists. By embracing gratitude and maintaining a positive outlook, we enhance our overall well-being, attract abundance, and approach life with a renewed sense of purpose and possibility.

Within the realm of travel is the potential to realize your dreams. As you venture into uncharted territories and face new challenges, you cultivate resilience, determination, and a growth mindset. The obstacles you overcome become stepping stones toward the realization of your dreams. Whether it is climbing a mountain, starting a business in a foreign land, or pursuing a passion project, travel empowers you to take bold action and create the life you envision. Embrace the spirit of adventure, for it is through the pursuit of your dreams that you will truly discover the heights of personal growth and success.

CHAPTER TWENTY-ONE

———

BRINGING THE JOURNEY HOME

Transitioning and Incorporating Your Experiences into Daily Life

Welcome back! It's time to embark on a new adventure—the journey of returning home. We've journeyed far and wide, embarked on incredible adventures, traversing uncharted territory and expanding our horizons. We've tasted the exotic flavors, breathed in the foreign air, and immersed ourselves in the captivating beauty of the countless destinations. After this delightful collection of whirlwind adventures, you may find yourself in a place where you want to plant some roots once again. This may mean returning to the place from which you started your epic remote-work-fueled voyage, a place you grew up in that harbors fond memories and old friends, or perhaps even a place you discovered along your journey that resonates deeply with your spirit. Whatever the case, there are some elements to consider when transitioning back to a life that is settled after a lengthy escapades on the road.

It's time to build a home and bring the essence of our travels into our everyday lives. We'll explore the process of integrating your journey into your daily life and ensuring that the transformative power of your travels continues to shape your path. I'll share some tips and insights on transitioning back to a settled lifestyle and infusing the lessons and experiences gained from your journey into your daily routines.

Transitioning Back to Settled Life: As you step back into the familiar, it's important to approach this transition with intention and grace. The key is to embrace this transition with an open mind and heart. Take some time to readjust, reconnect with friends and loved ones, and make conscious decisions regarding your new normal. Take a moment to reflect on the experiences you've had and the lessons you've learned. What have these journeys revealed about yourself and the world? Use this self-awareness as a compass to guide your reentry into settled life.

Coming home after an epic journey can be a mixed bag of emotions. On one hand, you're excited to reunite with loved ones and bask in the familiar comforts. On the other hand, you might feel a tinge of nostalgia for the incredible sights, sounds, and people you encountered on the road. You might even feel a pang of restlessness. It's a unique blend of emotions that calls for a delicate balance.

Recognize that vulnerability is not a weakness but a strength. It takes courage to acknowledge the longing for new experiences and the discomfort of readjusting to a familiar environment. Allow yourself to sit with these emotions and experience them fully. Reflect on how your journey has changed you, and share your vulnerability with trusted loved ones who can provide support and understanding. Take some time to acclimate yourself back to the rhythm of everyday life. Reconnect with family and friends, and let them in on your wild tales. Allow yourself to relish the joy of being home while staying open to the lessons that await you.

Incorporating Lessons and Experiences: Now, let's talk about how we can take the lessons and experiences gained from our travels and weave them into the fabric of our everyday lives. The first step is reflection—take some time to reflect on your journey—every step, every encounter, and every insight that has shaped you. Ask yourself: How have these experiences shaped me? What new perspectives and values have I acquired? How has my mindset evolved? What beliefs have I let go of, and what empowering beliefs have taken their place? By acknowledging the transformation within you, you gain a deeper understanding of the lessons you can apply in your daily choices and actions.

It's essential to be intentional about sharing your experiences with others. Engage in conversations that transcend the surface level, where you can share insights from your journeys. Share the moments that impacted you the most—the encounters, the challenges, and the epiphanies. Convey the experiences that touched your soul, the challenges that tested your mettle, and the moments that made you question everything.

Let the stories flow like a raging river, and allow the magic of your adventures to ignite the imagination of those around you. Let your experiences become a catalyst for connection, understanding, and inspiration. Allow your stories to inspire and uplift those around you, igniting a spark of curiosity and a thirst for exploration. Maybe even write a book about how to quit your desk job, embrace remote work, and travel the world. Remember, your experiences hold the power to broaden horizons and plant seeds of change in the hearts of others, encouraging them to explore the world in their own way.

But don't stop there. Incorporating your travels into daily life goes beyond storytelling. It's about embodying the lessons learned. Begin by distilling the wisdom you've acquired. Reflect on the landscapes that left you breathless and the cultures that expanded your understanding. Reminisce on the cultural nuances, the encounters with different perspectives, and the moments of personal growth. What values and principles have resonated with you? How can you integrate them into your daily routines and decision-making?

Infuse the spirit of your travels into your daily activities. Cook meals inspired by the flavors of the places you've visited, play music that evokes memories of distant lands, and decorate your space with souvenirs that remind you of your journeys. Let the sights, sounds, tastes, and aromas of your adventures become commonplace.

The adventure mindset becomes a way of life that permeates our every interaction and fuels our growth. Try new hobbies, seek out novel experiences, and embrace spontaneity. Make an active effort to find opportunities to engage with diverse communities in your backyard and continue to expand your horizons. It's about stepping to the edge of our comfort zones, where the unknown awaits. Venturing into uncharted territories, whether they're physical or metaphorical, and challenging ourselves to grow and evolve.

Be intentional about incorporating new practices and perspectives into your life. If you discovered a greater appreciation for simplicity and mindfulness, find ways to intertwine those qualities into your daily activities. If you feel deeply connected with a particular culture, explore ways to celebrate and honor it in your home. Cultivate a sense of curiosity and openness, even when you're not physically on the road. You can actively weave the spirit of adventure in everyday life by embracing change and approaching challenges enthusiastically.

As you settle back into the familiarity of your home, it's vital to keep the flame of adventure burning bright. The journey doesn't end when you unpack your bags. The more you embrace the spirit of adventure, the more doors of opportunity will open, leading you closer to success. The adventure doesn't stop—it simply takes on a different form. Explore your local community with fresh eyes, venture into unexplored territories of your hometown, uncover hidden gems, engage with like-minded souls, and dive into activities that ignite your passion. Embrace the mindset of constant improvement, seeking opportunities for growth and expansion in every area of your life. Celebrate your progress, no matter how small, and use it as fuel to propel you forward.

Just as you embrace a growth mindset during your travels, continue to nurture that mindset as you settle back into your daily life, no matter where you are. Embrace the profound shift in your perception and identity, recognizing that you are not the same person who left home. Allow yourself to fully lean into the changes that have occurred within you and recognize the immense value they hold.

Now that you've gained a deeper understanding of who you are and what you value, it's time to craft a personal vision for your future. Set aside time to clarify your goals, aspirations, and dreams. Imagine the life you want to create and visualize it vividly. As you do so, let go of any limiting beliefs or doubts that may hold you back. Embrace the belief that you have the power to shape your world and make your dreams a tangible reality.

Returning home, even for a season, allows you to evaluate your current situation and set new goals aligned with the person you've become through your travels. Take the time to define your aspirations and craft a clear plan that reflects the lessons learned and the experiences gained during your journey.

With your vision in place, break down your goals into smaller, manageable and actionable steps. Align those actions with your values and purpose, ensuring that each step brings you closer to your desired outcomes. Remember, just like when you're on the road, it's not just about the destination but the journey itself. Stay committed to the process, embrace a growth mindset, and seek continuous improvement in all areas—personal, professional, and spiritual.

Returning home can sometimes feel isolating, especially when others may not fully understand or appreciate your transformation. Be patient with yourself and those around you, understanding that everyone navigates change differently. Seek support from loved ones who can provide encouragement, and remember to extend compassion to yourself.

Align yourself with like-minded individuals who share your

passion for personal development and success and can guide and support you along the way. By surrounding yourself with a supportive community, you gain valuable insights, accountability, and inspiration to keep pushing forward. Together, you can uplift and inspire one another as you navigate the path of reintegration.

While traveling opens our eyes to new horizons, there is also great beauty in returning to the place we call home. Take the time to appreciate the familiarity, the comfort, and the connections that await you. Rediscover the magic of your hometown, the warmth of family and friends, and the simple joys of everyday life. You can find a renewed appreciation for the place you once left behind by approaching your homecoming with gratitude and an open heart.

Embracing home does not mean leaving our adventures behind; it means carrying them within us, allowing them to shape our perspectives and actions. Transition with intention, share your stories, embody the lessons learned, and keep the flame of curiosity alive, even in the familiar. Stay committed to your vision, take aligned, intentional action, and surround yourself with a supportive community.

As we wrap this chapter up, remember that our travels have left an indelible mark on our souls. It is not the end of your journey but rather the beginning of a new one filled with limitless possibilities. We've grown, learned, and expanded our perspectives in ways we could have never imagined. Now, it's time to bring that spirit of adventure and enlightenment into our settled lives. Through your continued growth and expansion, you have the power to create a life that is authentically yours—one that reflects the profound transformation you've experienced on your travels.

Besides, there is no stopping you from packing your bags and heading back out on the road. You did it once, and you can do it again. Whenever you want, grab your passport, charge up your laptop, and embark on this remarkable journey of remote work and travel. You've got the tools, the mindset, and the hunger for success. It's time to make the most of every mile traveled and every task accomplished. Let your dreams unfold before your very eyes, my friend. The world is your canvas, and with the right mindset and actions, you can create a masterpiece of success and personal achievement, whether at home or abroad.

ABOUT THE AUTHOR

Aaron Clements is a multifaceted individual, embodying the roles of an investor, business and life coach, bestselling author, singer, songwriter, entrepreneur, and digital nomad. His lifestyle reflects a deep commitment to travel, typically spending around 300 days a year on the road. This nomadic existence is made possible by his adept management of multiple business ventures that can be run from anywhere in the world.

Aaron's success lies in his ability to craft a life that harmonizes his passions and professional endeavors. He is driven by a desire to share his experiences and knowledge, inspiring others to break free from conventional corporate constraints and embrace a life of travel and adventure. Through his work, Aaron seeks to empower individuals to pursue their dreams, demonstrating that with positivity, determination, and a global perspective, one can create a fulfilling and impactful lifestyle.

Despite his jet-setting lifestyle, Aaron remains grounded in his personal life. He values time spent with his mother and does his part to support the food-insecure population of his hometown. This commitment to community and family underscores his belief in using his success to improve the lives of others.

When he's not backstage at concerts or enjoying the serenity of a beach, Aaron can be found engaging with his audience on his website, www.AaronBClements.com and social media platforms. He invites people to connect with him to explore how they too can live a life that blends passion, purpose, and adventure. Aaron currently calls Indianapolis, IN home, and his spirit is one of boundless exploration and a commitment to living life to the fullest.

Printed in Great Britain
by Amazon

43515148R00086